The Field Guide to Vintage

Farm Tractors

Text by Robert N. Pripps

Photographs by Andrew Morland

Voyageur Press

A TOWN SQUARE BOOK

Dedication

For my daughters-in-law, Andrea, Beth, and Julie

Text copyright © 1999 by Robert N. Pripps
Photographs copyright © 1999 by Andrew Morland and other photographers where noted
Illustration on front cover and page one © 1998 Kristy Tucker

Edited by Michael Dregni
Designed by Andrea Rud
Printed in Hong Kong
00   01   02   03   04   6   5   4   3   2

Library of Congress Cataloging-in-Publication Data
    The field guide to vintage farm tractors / text by Robert N. Pripps ;
photography by Andrew Morland.
      p.   cm.
    Includes bibliographical references and index.
    ISBN 0-89658-365-1
    1. Farm tractors—Collectors and collecting. 2. Farm tractors—Pictorial works.
I. Title.
    TL233.25.P75   1999
    629.225'2—dc21   98-31448
                                CIP

Distributed in Canada by Raincoast Books, 9050 Shaughnessy Street, Vancouver, B.C. V6P 6E5

Distributed in Europe by Midland Publishing Ltd.
24 The Hollow, Earl Shilton, Leicester LE9 7NA, England
Tel: 01455 233747

Published by Voyageur Press, Inc.
123 North Second Street, P.O. Box 338, Stillwater, MN 55082 U.S.A.
651-430-2210, fax 651-430-2211

Educators, fundraisers, premium and gift buyers, publicists, and marketing managers: Looking for creative products and new sales ideas? Voyageur Press books are available at special discounts when purchased in quantities, and special editions can be created to your specifications. For details contact the marketing department at 800-888-9653.

Page 1: *A rare International Harvester Farmall AV High Crop.*

Contents

Introduction

Interest in vintage farm tractors has swept the world in the last decade. Perhaps it's because almost all of us have some nostalgic connection to tractors, or perhaps it's because we see things changing so rapidly right in front of our eyes that we want to hang on to a bit of the past.

Author Robert N. Pripps on his 1948 John Deere Model B.

Another theory is that in this day of computer-aided design, competing products are losing traits of individuality; in other words, everyone is using the same software program and getting the same results. This was certainly not so when these tractors were first developed. The personalities of the designers came through, and now these machines are like moving memorials to them and their place in history.

Whatever the reason, I hope this book will add to the interest in and the understanding of these great old machines. I have tried to present a thumb-nail sketch of the tractors most often collected and restored, up to around 1960. My friend and legendary automotive photographer Andrew Morland has provided one or two photos of each classification.

No doubt we missed somebody's favorite. Also, no doubt, there may be some technical errors; please convey any corrections or additions to me through the publisher and we will incorporate them.

A word of thanks is in order to the owners of the beautifully restored tractors shown on these pages. Space restrictions in the captions generally precluded giving credit to the owners and restorers. In many cases, these collectors went to a lot of trouble getting their machines out and moving them around to capture the best light.

My thanks as well to Bob LaVoie for his help with Caterpillar images.

Another word of thanks to Voyageur Press for bravely undertaking this project, and to the managers, designers, editors, and others who get these books out to the far corners of the world. A special thanks to Editorial Director Michael Dregni whose idea it was to publish *The Field Guide to Vintage Farm Tractors*.

Robert N. Pripps
Springstead, Wisconsin
1998

A Model 11/22 made by Sawyer-Massey.

Two Huber Super Fours (20/40), also known as Model HKs.

A John Deere Model LA. (Photograph by Robert N. Pripps)

A diesel-powered Ferguson TE-20 with a Ferguson two-way plow. Ferguson was noted for innovative implements to complement the abilities of the "Fergie" tractor.

Advance-Rumely Thresher Company
LaPorte, Indiana, USA

Advance-Rumely OilPull

The OilPull line of tractors began in 1909 when Dr. Edward Rumely, grandson of the company founder, collaborated with John Secor, who had been doing engine experiments for more than twenty years. They developed a line of one- and two-cylinder tractors that used oil, rather than water, as an engine coolant. The oil, with its higher boiling point, allowed higher engine temperatures for more efficient use of the low-volatility kerosene fuel. Engine cylinders were offset from the crankshaft centerline to reduce piston side loads. The engines used water injection, sometimes consuming as much water as fuel. Cooling oil was circulated by a centrifugal pump. Engine exhaust was used to induce airflow through the chimney-type radiator. After 1918, high-tension magneto ignitions were used, beginning as an extra-cost option. The tractors were driven through an expanding shoe clutch and a spur-gear final drive. One-, two-, and three-speed transmissions were used.

The OilPull line was noted for its large-displacement, slow-turning engines. OilPull tractors could generally best their official power and pull ratings, a fact that endeared them to their owners.

Models and Variations

Model	Years Built	Model	Years Built
25/45 Type B	1910–1914	25/45 Type R	1924–1927
15/30 Type C	1911–1917	20/35 Type M	1924–1927
	(one-cylinder)	15/25 Type L	1924–1927 (first
18/35 Type D	1918–1918		locking differential)
	(one-cylinder)	30/60 Type S	1924–1928
30/60 Type E	1911–1923	20/30 Type W	1928–1930
14/28 Type F	1918–1919	25/40 Type X	1928–1930
16/30 Type F	1919–1924	30/50 Type Y	1928–1930
12/20 Type K	1919–1924	40/60 Type Z	1929–1930
20/40 Type G	1920–1924		

Specifications:
Advance-Rumely 25/45 Type R

Engine: Overhead-valve two-cylinder
Bore & stroke: 7.81x9.50 inches
  (195.25x237.5 mm)
Displacement: 911 ci (14,922 cc)

Power: 45 hp
Transmission: Three speeds forward
Weight: 13,000 pounds (5,850 kg)

A 1920 Advance-Rumely OilPull Type F, which was rated at 16 drawbar and 30 belt hp. The "OilPull" name signified that oil was used as a coolant.

The Advance-Rumely OilPull Type Z carried a rating of 40 drawbar and 60 belt hp. Owner: Don Wolf of Fort Wayne, Indiana.

Advance-Rumely 6

"A four plow tractor at the weight of a three, a six-cylinder at the price of a four," touted the advertisements of the time for the standard-tread Rumely 6 (sometimes called the 6A). It was launched in 1930, about the same time Advance-Rumely was acquired by Allis-Chalmers. The Rumely 6 remained in Allis-Chalmers's catalogs until 1934, however, and more than 800 of these modern tractors were made. The Rumely 6 was a capable and competitive machine with its smooth six-cylinder engine easily pulling four 14-inch (35-cm) plows.

A 1930 Rumely 6. Although production of this type ended in 1931, it stayed in the Allis-Chalmers catalog until the last existing units were sold in 1934.

Models and Variations

Model	Years Built
6 (6A)	1930–1934

Specifications: Advance-Rumely 6A

Engine: L-head four-cylinder
Bore & stroke: 4.25x4.75 inches
   (106.25x118.75 mm)
Displacement: 404 ci (6,618 cc)
Rating: 48 belt hp
Transmission: Six speeds forward, two
   speeds reverse
Weight: 6,000 pounds (2,700 kg)

Production of the Rumely 6 began in 1930 and ended in 1931 when Advance-Rumely was taken over by Allis-Chalmers. Owner: Royce Schultz of Monroe, Wisconsin.

Albaugh-Dover Company
Chicago, Illinois, USA

Albaugh-Dover Square Turn

Albaugh-Dover was a noted Chicago mail-order company in the first decades of the twentieth century. In 1916, Albaugh-Dover bought out the Kenney-Colwell Company of Norfolk, Nebraska, which had developed an unconventional tractor called the K.C. Albaugh-Dover renamed the machine the "Square Turn"; later, the entire company was renamed the Square Turn Tractor Company, based in Chicago.

Variously rated at 15/30, 18/30, and 18/35 hp, the tractor employed a unique drive system. Power from the engine was transmitted into a dual-cone-drive transmission with a cone to drive each main wheel. Speed was continuously variable up to 3 mph (4.8 km/h) in either forward or reverse. Through a system of levers and chain, the cones were used in conjunction with the single rear (steering) wheel, so that one drive wheel rotated forward and the other in reverse, thereby making a "square turn." The Square Turn also featured Bennett dual carburetors, splash lubrication, and fan cooling with the aid of a water pump. The company survived until 1925.

Models and Variations	
Model	Years Built
Square Turn	1916–1925

Specifications:
Albaugh-Dover Square Turn
Engine: Climax four-cylinder
Displacement: 510 ci (8,354 cc)
Rating: 15 drawbar hp, 30 belt hp (early),
  18/35 hp (late)
Weight: 7,400 pounds (3,330 kg)

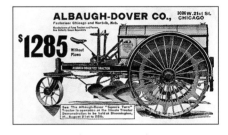

Advertisement for the Albaugh-Dover Square Turn.

The Albaugh-Dover Square Turn featured a unique transmission using dual cone drives that allowed one drive wheel to go forward while the other went backward. Thus the Square Turn could make square turns. Owner: Kurt Umnus.

Allis-Chalmers Company
Milwaukee, Wisconsin, USA

Allis-Chalmers Model 10/18

The Allis-Chalmers Company was formed in 1901, although its roots can be traced back to 1847. The firm was involved in steam power, sawmill gear, flour-milling equipment, as well as the manufacture of electrical paraphernalia. The Model 10/18 was the first tractor from Allis-Chalmers, introduced in 1914. General Otto Falk, president of A-C, decided the rapidly expanding farm tractor market held possibilities for the company.

The 10/18 had an unusual three-wheel configuration, with the single front wheel offset to be in line with the right rear wheel. The 10/18 was remarkably small and light compared with most tractors of the period, which more closely favored their steam-engine ancestry. The 10/18 boasted a one-piece steel frame, a two-cylinder horizontally opposed engine, a belt pulley, and operated on kerosene. It offered one forward and one reverse speed, but could manage three 14-inch (35-cm) plows under favorable conditions. About 2,700 Model 10/18s were delivered.

Right: Built in the Milwaukee suburb of West Allis, Wisconsin, the Model 10/18 was the first Allis-Chalmers tractor. Advertising copy boasted of a one-piece frame that would not sag. Owner: Norm Meinert of Davis, Illinois.

Below: The largest Allis-Chalmers in the 1920s was the rare 20/35 with its 461-ci (7,600-cc) engine developing up to 45 hp.

Models and Variations	
Model	Years Built
10/18	1914–1921

Specifications:
Allis-Chalmers Model 10/18

Engine: Horizontally opposed two-cylinder
Bore & stroke: 5.25x7.00 inches
   (131.25x175 mm)
Displacement: 303 ci (4,963 cc)
Power: 18 belt hp
Transmission: One speed forward
Weight: 4,800 pounds (2,160 kg)

Allis-Chalmers Model 6/12

The diminutive Model 6/12 was essentially a copy of the remarkably innovative Moline Universal. The 6/12 had only two wheels: It relied on a trailing sulky or a wheeled implement to carry the back end. Like the Universal, the 6/12 employed articulated steering with a center hinge between the implement and the tractor. Neither the 6/12 nor the Moline Universal found great acceptance by farmers of the period, primarily because of the time and effort required to change implements.

The 6/12 used a well-respected four-cylinder engine from LeRoi, also of Milwaukee. The LeRoi engine was equipped with an air cleaner, a unique feature for the time. The 6/12 also boasted a belt pulley mounted on the aft end of the engine, parallel to the engine centerline. Drive belts could not be tightened in the usual fashion by backing the tractor; instead, the belt was tightened, after reasonably accurate placement of the tractor, by steering the tractor to swing the pulley away from the driven load. The 6/12 was rated for two ten-inch (25-cm) plows.

Models and Variations	
Model	Years Built
6/12	1919–1926

Specifications:
Allis-Chalmers Model 6/12
Engine: LeRoi Model 2C side-valve four-cylinder
Bore & stroke: 3.125x4.50 inches (78x112.5 mm)
Displacement: 138 ci (2,260 cc)
Power: 6 drawbar hp, 12 belt hp

$1,500,000 Have Been Spent in the Past Four Years to make Allis-Chalmers Farm Tractors Right for You

Advertisement for the Allis-Chalmers 6/12: "$1,500,000 Have Been Spent in the Past Four Years to make Allis-Chalmers Farm Tractors Right for You."

The 1919 Allis-Chalmers 6/12 was an early attempt at an all-purpose tractor. The sulky plow, shown here, could be replaced with a variety of implements, including a road grader.

Above: *Allis-Chalmers exported some of its Model U tractors through channels forged for its industrial products; this 1936 Model U is owned by Alan Draper of Great Britain.*

Left: *The Allis-Chalmers Model UC was the row-crop version of the famous Model U. This a 1935 vintage machine.*

Allis–Chalmers
Models U and UC

The Allis-Chalmers Model U tractor has the distinction of being the first farm tractor to be offered for sale with low-pressure pneumatic rubber tires. Its row-crop running mate, the UC, was equipped with a power lift for its clever drive-in cultivator.

The Model U was initially designed and manufactured in 1929 by Allis-Chalmers for the United Tractor and Equipment Corporation of Chicago. United also folded in 1929, so A-C offered the tractor to its dealers as the Allis-Chalmers United. The next year the designation was changed to the Model U. The first 7,404 Model Us made used a Continental flathead four-cylinder engine; subsequent units were equipped with Allis's own overhead-valve four. The U, UC, and subsequent Allis-Chalmers tractors were painted Persian Orange.

The Model U also has the distinction of being a speedy tractor. To introduce rubber tires, special versions of the U were prepared for demonstrations at state fairs and other venues and driven by famous race drivers; Ab Jenkins attained a record 67 mph (107 km/h) driving a Model U on the Bonneville Salt Flats in Utah.

Models and Variations		Specifications:
Model	**Years Built**	**1935 Allis-Chalmers Model U**
United	1929	Engine: Overhead-valve four-cylinder
U	1930–1932 (Continental)	Bore & stroke: 4.375x5.00 inches (109.375x125 mm); after 1936,
U	1933–1944 (Allis-Chalmers)	4.50x5.00 (112.5x125 mm) Displacement: 300 ci (4,914 cc); 284 ci
UC	1930–1932 (Continental)	(4,652 cc) for Continental Power: 33 belt hp
UC	1933–1941 (Allis-Chalmers)	Transmission: Four speeds forward Weight: 5,140 pounds (2,313 kg)

Allis-Chalmers Models WC, WF, WD, WD-45, WD-45D

The two-plow WC was introduced in 1933. It was the first tractor to be offered with rubber tires as standard equipment; steel wheels were optional. It employed a channel frame, which was lighter and less expensive than the castings used on the Model U; the WC weighed only 3,200 pounds (1,440 kg). The 201-ci (3,292-cc) engine featured a 4.00x4.00-inch (100x100-mm) bore and stroke, and was rated at 1,300 rpm. Both kerosene and gasoline versions were available. The WC was a row-crop tractor; its standard-tread running mate, the WF, was introduced in 1940 and produced through 1951. Allis-Chalmers built more than 186,000 WC and WF tractors.

The popular WC was succeeded by the WD in 1948. The WD boasted the first power-adjustable rear wheel tread and was also one of the first tractors available with a live power takeoff (PTO). The same engine was used as in the WC, but the WD's rated speed was upped to 1,400 rpm. The WD was available in dual-tricycle, single, and adjustable wide front ends.

The WD was followed in 1953 by the WD-45, built along the same lines. The engine of the WD-45 had a 4.50-inch (112.5-mm) stroke, giving it substantially more power. It was available in gasoline, dual-fuel, and LPG versions. In 1955, the WD-45D six-cylinder diesel was offered.

Right: *An Allis-Chalmers WC runs a large Allis-Chalmers All-Crop PTO-driven combine.*

Below: *In 1955, Allis-Chalmers introduced the WD-45 Diesel. It was powered by a 230-ci (3,767-cc), six-cylinder engine that produced 40 hp. Owner: Theodore Buisker of Davis, Illinois.*

Left: *An Allis-Chalmers WC with an Allis-Chalmers bale loader, which was designed to pick up bales left in the field by the Allis-Chalmers Roto-Baler.*

Below: *The Allis-Chalmers WD-45 lineup, featuring diesel, LPG, and gasoline versions of the workhorse tractor.*

Models and Variations

Model	Years Built
WC	1933–1948
WF	1940–1951
WD	1948–1953
WD-45	1953–1957
WD-45D	1955–1957

Specifications:
Allis-Chalmers WD-45

Engine: Overhead-valve four-cylinder
Bore & stroke: 4.00x4.50 inches
   (100x112.5 mm)
Displacement: 226 ci (3,702 cc)
Power: 39 belt hp
Transmission: Four speeds forward
Weight: 4,000 pounds (1,800 kg)

The Allis-Chalmers Model WF was the standard-tread version of the more common Model WC. This one sports a nifty umbrella.

A nicely restored 1949 Allis-Chalmers WD. It featured power-adjustable rear wheels and a live PTO. Allis-Chalmers sold more than 160,000 WD tractors between 1948 and 1953.

Allis-Chalmers Model G

The compact Allis-Chalmers Model G used a four-cylinder Continental engine that was virtually the same engine as in the Farmall Cub.

The Allis-Chalmers G is unique in the annals of vintage tractors. First introduced in 1948 as a "hoe on wheels" for truck gardeners, the most distinctive feature of the G was its rear-mounted, 10-hp four-cylinder Continental engine. The operator's seat was ahead of the engine. Tubular frame members extended forward, locating the front wheels and providing a mounting place for a variety of implements. Visibility, especially for guiding the cultivator, was unimpeded. Even the steering wheel had a segment of the rim omitted, much like an airplane control wheel, to avoid blocking the view. The three-speed transmission could be obtained with a special low-speed first gear for cultivating delicate plants at less than one mph (1.6 km/h). Because of its uniqueness and because only 30,000 were made, the Allis-Chalmers Model G is much sought after by collectors. The special low gear makes them popular for "slow races," as well.

Models and Variations

Model	Years Built
G	1948-1955

Specifications:
Allis-Chalmers Model G

Engine: L-head four-cylinder Continental
Bore & stroke: 2.375x3.50 inches
   (59.375x87.5 mm)
Displacement: 62 ci (1,016 cc)
Power: 10 hp
Transmission: Three speeds forward
Weight: 1,550 pounds (697.5 kg)

The unique Allis-Chalmers Model G was introduced in 1948 and produced through 1955 for nurserymen and truck gardeners, yet only about 30,000 were sold during that time.

Allis-Chalmers Models B, C, CA

In response to the successful Farmall F-12, Allis-Chalmers introduced its small, inexpensive Model B in 1938. It was a one-plow machine weighing less than one ton (90 kg) and featuring a wide-front arched axle. It was designed as a replacement for the teams of horses, which still provided most of the motive power for pre–World War II farms. Front and rear tread were adjustable by reversing wheels and by changing wheel clamps; a fully adjustable front axle was available later. With rubber tires and an electrical system, the Allis B, as it was affectionately called, sold for less than $600.

Similar to the B, the Model C had a tricycle front end and—as its bore was increased to 3.375 inches (84.375 mm)—a slightly more powerful engine. In 1949, a Model CA was introduced with the governor set to a maximum 1,650 rpm rather than 1,500 rpm. The CA had a four-speed, rather than three-speed, transmission.

Models and Variations

Model	Years Built
B	1938–1958
C	1939–1949
CA	1949–1958

Specifications:
Allis-Chalmers Model B

Engine: Overhead-valve four-cylinder
Bore & stroke: 3.25x3.50 inches
    (81.25x87.5 mm)
Displacement: 116 ci (1,900 cc)
Power: 16 belt hp
Transmission: Three speeds forward
Weight: 1,900 pounds (855 kg)

Above, top: More than 84,000 Allis-Chalmers Model C tractors were delivered between 1939 and 1949. This one has the more rare "donut" single front wheel.

Above, bottom: One of niftiest little tractors made, the Allis-Chalmers Model B was rated at 16 belt hp. The arched front axle allowed the B to straddle a row. Shown is a 1942 version.

Left: A 1939 Allis-Chalmers Model B. Even though it was lightweight, the B was capable of serious work. When introduced in 1938, it cost less than $500.

Allis-Chalmers Model D-17

The gasoline-powered Series IV Allis-Chalmers D-17 of 1965–1967 is one of the most popular, capable, and collectible of the Allis-Chalmers tractors.

Between 1957 and 1960, Allis-Chalmers revised its entire line of tractors to make them more stylish and competitive. The most popular of these—and the most collectible today—was the Model D-17. This truly remarkable tractor used an engine with the same dimensions as the WD-45, but obtained almost 60 hp on LPG fuel. Gasoline and a six-cylinder diesel were also available. Other interesting features were the Roll-Shift front-axle tread adjusting system that utilized the power steering to affect the change. The D-17 also had as standard equipment the Power-Director, a power shift high-low range selector.

The D-17 was produced in four series, with trim and decals as the only differences. The Series IV, however, was the only one available with a regular three-point hitch. The Model D-17 was available with single and dual-tricycle fronts as well as the power-adjustable wide front. Wheatland and orchard fenders were options. Because of its wide stance and low center of gravity, the D-17 made a great endloader tractor.

Models and Variations		Specifications:
Model	Years Built	Allis-Chalmers D-17 Gasoline
D-17	1957–1959	Engine: Overhead-valve four-cylinder
Series II	1959–1964	Bore & stroke: 4.00x4.50 inches
Series III	1964–1965	(100x112.5 mm)
Series IV	1965–1967	Displacement: 226 ci (3,702 cc)
		Power: 50 belt hp
		Transmission: Eight speeds forward
		Weight: 4,700 pounds (2,115 kg)

Avery Company
Peoria, Illinois, USA

Avery Horizontally Opposed Models

The Avery 40/80 was a 22,000-pound (9,900-kg) monster that used two Model 22/35 engines hooked together. It was rerated as a 45/65 after it failed to live up to its claims.

Not to be confused with the B. F. Avery Company of Louisville, Kentucky, this Avery Company was founded in 1874, in Galesburg, Illinois, to manufacture corn planters. The firm moved to Peoria in 1884. Avery's first internal-combustion tractor was a combination tractor-truck, introduced in 1909, but it was not a success; Avery's second attempt, a giant single-cylinder machine, also failed.

Avery then created a series of horizontally opposed two- and four-cylinder tractors that gained a reputation for dependability. Draft exhaust with a cylindrical chimney was a characteristic of this series.

Advertisement showing the Avery lineup, from the small 5/10 to the monster 40/80.

Models and Variations

Model	Year Built
20/35	1912–1915
40/80	1913–1920 (two 20/35 engines put together)
12/25	1912–1919
8/16	1914–1922 ("half-scale" version of 20/35)
25/50	1914–1922 (two 12/25 engines put together)
18/36	1916–1921 (two 8/16 engines put together; first tractor to use engine sleeves)
14/28	1919–1924 (four-cylinder)
45/65	1920–1924

Specifications: Avery 40/80
Engine: Horizontally opposed four-cylinder
Bore & stroke: 7.75x8.00 inches (193.75x200 mm)
Displacement: 1,509 ci (24,717 cc)
Rating: 40 drawbar hp, 80 belt hp; rerated 45/65 as the result of Nebraska Tractor Test #44
Transmission: Two speeds forward
Weight: 22,000 pounds (9,900 kg)

J. I. Case Company Inc.

Racine, Wisconsin, USA

Case Models 30/60, 20/40, 12/25

Jerome Increase Case was one of several geniuses of the nineteenth century who had a profound impact on agriculture—and on society in general. Case founded his business, the J. I. Case Threshing Machine Company, in 1843, when he was just twenty-four years old. Within five years, the company was the largest employer in the newly formed state of Wisconsin. Case's company, which absorbed many important competitors over the years (including International Harvester), is still headquartered in Racine, Wisconsin. It is now one of the four largest agricultural-equipment manufacturers in the world.

A 1912 Case 20/40 gas/kerosene tractor runs a threshing machine via its belt pulley.

Case became the largest producer of steam engines between 1870 and 1925; inevitably the company developed internal-combustion tractors. Case's first attempt, known as the Patterson Gas Tractor (named for the brothers who invented the engine), was built in 1892. Carburetor and ignition difficulties forced postponement of further tractor activities until 1910.

The first in the ensuing production series of two-cylinder Case tractors was the 30/60. It had a four-cycle engine, hot-riveted frame, two-speed transmission, and exhaust-draft cooling. Following in short order was the 20/40 with the same general configuration. Next came the 12/25 with a similar, but smaller, engine and transmission, as well as a conventional radiator and fan.

Models and Variations

Model	Years Built
30/60	1912–1916
20/40	1912–1917
12/25	1914–1918

Specifications: Case Model 20/40

Engine: Overhead-valve two-cylinder
Bore & stroke: 7.75x8.00 inches
  (193.75x200 mm)
Displacement: 755 ci (12,367 cc)
Power: 20 drawbar hp, 40 belt hp
Transmission: Two speeds forward
Weight: 13,000 pounds (5,850 kg)

Case Crossmotors 10/20 and 9/18

By the 1910s, Case recognized the trend toward smaller, lighter, cheaper tractors. During this period, three-wheel configurations were becoming popular; the theory was that traction could be improved if the differential was eliminated from the drivetrain. Case's approach with the Model 10/20 was unique, however: It had two driving wheels in back and only one front wheel, in line with the right rear. The left rear wheel was ordinarily not connected to the drive, except in hard going. Then it could be clutched in directly (without a differential) for straight-line pulling. This tractor used a variation of the Case automobile engine mounted with the cylinders vertical but with its crankshaft crosswise to the direction of travel.

The 9/18 tractor used a similar engine configuration, but with a conventional four-wheel arrangement with a sloping hood and a radiator in front. Differential gearing was located in the left wheel hub covered by a sheet-metal cover. The 9/18 used round-spoke wheels.

Above: *A 1916 Case 9/18. More than 6,000 were shipped between 1916 and 1918. The unusual, fully enclosed hood made the 9/18 an attractive machine. The drive gears were still exposed, however.*

Models and Variations	
Model	Years Built
10/20	1915-1922
9/18	1916-1918

Specifications: Case Model 10/20
Engine: Overhead-valve four-cylinder
Bore & stroke: 4.25x6.00 inches (106x150 mm)
Displacement: 341 ci (5,586 cc)
Power: 20 belt hp
Transmission: One speed forward
Weight: 5,000 pounds (2,250 kg)

Right: *The Case 10/18 had three wheels arranged like those of the Allis-Chalmers 10/18, except the Case used a clutch for the left rear wheel rather than a differential. Shown is a 1918 model.*

Case Crossmotors 9/18B, 10/18, 12/20, 15/27, 22/40, 40/72

A 15/27 Case Model K of 1920 vintage. The 15/27 had two front-axle pivot holes, and the axle could be shifted to the right for the front wheel to run in the furrow while the right rear wheel ran on unplowed ground.

A revised 9/18B tractor was introduced in 1918, when the awesome competitive on-slaught of the Fordson was recognized. The riveted sheet-metal frame was replaced by a single cast unit that provided housing for the engine crankshaft and all the gears. This tractor also differed from the previous 9/18 in that it had flat-spoke wheels and a flat, rather than a sloping, hood. Almost immediately after introduction, the engine speed was upped 150 rpm and the tractor was redesignated the 10/18. Later, the tractor was lengthened 7.5 inches (18.75 cm) and the power increased. It then became the 12/20, or Model A.

The third in this series was the upscaled 15/27, which also went by the designations 18/32 and Model K. This tractor differed visually from the smaller models mainly in that the exhaust pipe was bent to the left to direct the gasses away from the operator.

In the early 1920s, Case was delivering large threshers and to provide the power required, the massive 22/40 and 40/72 were offered. The torque of these powerhouses required a return to the older hot-riveted, channel-iron frames.

Models and Variations		Specifications: Case Model 15/27
Model	Years Built	Engine: Overhead-valve four-cylinder
9/18B	1918–1918	Bore & stroke: 4.50x6.00 inches
10/18	1918–1921	(112.5x150 mm)
12/20, A	1921–1928	Displacement: 382 ci (6,257 cc)
15/27, 18/32, K	1919–1928	Power: 32 hp in final, Model K version
22/40, 25/45, T	1919–1928	Transmission: Two speeds forward
40/72	1920–1923	Weight: 6,500 pounds (2,925 kg)

A 1919 Case 22/40.

A Case Model A 12/20 of about 1923 vintage. The Model A was Case's answer to the popular Fordson. It was like the earlier 10/18, but had a bore increase of 0.25 inches (6.25 mm).

Case Models L, LA, 500, 600, 900

In 1928, new Case president Leon Clausen ordered the entire line of Crossmotor tractors to be replaced by two models, the L and C. It was apparently a good decision as these models and their variations kept Case competitive for the next thirty years.

The Model L and it successors were characterized by a conventional standard-tread layout with the engine crank parallel to the line of travel, a hand clutch, and a chain final drive. The L featured a new "high-speed," 1,100-rpm, four-cylinder engine. The LA was introduced in 1940 along with the change of color from gray to Flambeau Red. It had stylish sheet metal, engine improvements, and a new four-speed transmission. An electrical system was optional, as was an LPG fuel version. Next came the Model LAD (LA Diesel) in 1952.

In the 1950s, the three-number system of identifiers was adopted, and the first model produced was designated the Model 500. The new diesel was Case's first six-cylinder. It also incorporated an optional live

Brochure for the Case Model L.

PTO. The 500 became the 600 in 1957, and it now sported Desert Sunset beige paint and a six-speed transmission. Power steering was now standard equipment. A six-cylinder LPG engine was also offered. The final version of the venerable Model L plowing tractor was the 900. It was the same as the 600, but with restyled sheet metal.

Models and Variations		Specifications: Case Model 600 Diesel
Model	Years Built	Engine: Overhead-valve six-cylinder
L	1928–1940	Bore & stroke: 4.00x5.00 inches
LA	1940–1953	(100x125 mm)
500	1953–1956	Displacement: 377 ci (6,175 cc)
600	1957–1957	Power: 70 hp
900	1957–1959	Transmission: Six speeds forward
		Weight: 8,000 pounds (3,600 kg)

Above, top: *This Case Model 500 was just in from plowing at the Great Dorset Steam Fair in England. It used a Case-built diesel of 377 ci (6,175 cc). It featured a main bearing between each connecting rod.*

Above, center: *The Case Model 600 was an upgrade of the Model 500. Besides getting a new six-speed transmission, the 600 now sported the Desert Sunset paint. It was built only in the 1957 model year.*

Above, bottom: *This 1959 Case Model 900 (910B) is powered by liquefied petroleum gas (LPG), a popular fuel in the late 1950s. It still retained the chain final drive pioneered in 1929 on the Model L.*

Above: *The Case Model L was one of the most powerful tractors of its day, with only Rumely and Minneapolis-Moline offering generally comparable tractors. This Model L dates from 1929. Owner: Jay Foxworthy of Washburn, Illinois.*

Left: *The Case Model LA replaced the venerable Model L in 1940. It was modernized on the outside, but retained many of the L's features under the skin. A 1951 Model LA is shown.*

Case Models C, CC, D, DC

A 1937 Case Model CC-3. This was the most popular of the C family, and it was available in either single- or dual-wheel tricycle front ends.

The Case Model C was a scaled-down version of the Model L—even to the roller-chain final drive. The C was available in a variety of configurations, including industrial, orchard, vineyard, sugar cane specials, and high clearance types, but the row-crop Model CC—available in the CC-3 and CC-4 versions—and the standard-tread Model C were far and away the most popular. The CC-3 was configured for adjustable front and rear wheel treads, or either a single- or dual-wheel tricycle arrangement. The CC-4 had fixed tread width, and was generally equipped with a standard-tread front axle. It was, however, field-convertible to a tricycle configuration. Rear wheel adjustment was accomplished by installing, or removing, various-length axle spools and by reversing the wheels. From 1935 on, the CC was available with Case's Motor Lift.

The Model D and its variations replaced the Model C in 1939 with the introduction of the restyled Flambeau Red Series. Under the new colorful skin was essentially the same tractor as the Model C. Row-crop DC-3 and DC-4 variants were the same as those of the earlier Model CC. Hydraulics was added to the D line in 1950. In 1952, the Eagle Hitch and LPG fuel options were added.

Models and Variations		Specifications: 1940 Case Model D
Model	Years Built	Engine: Overhead-valve four-cylinder
C	1929–1939	Bore & stroke: 3.875x5.50 inches
CC-3	1929–1939	(97x137.5 mm)
CC-4	1931–1938	Displacement: 260 ci (4,259 cc)
D	1939–1953	Power: 32 belt hp
DC-3	1939–1953	Transmission: Four speeds forward
DC-4	1939–1953	Weight: 7,000 pounds (3,150 kg)

The All-Purpose Case Model DC-3 was available with dual tricycle front wheels, as shown, or a single front wheel. This example has been converted to a 12-volt alternator electrical system.

The Model C Case was a scaled-down version of the Model L. The same tractor, but in row-crop configuration, was called the Model CC. John Davis of Maplewood, Ohio, owns this 1929 Model C.

Above: *A 1950 Case Model D pulling a Case Centinel 2x14-inch (2x35-mm) plow. Formerly in the service of the Kentucky Parks Department, it is now owned by Tom Graverson of Bremen, Indiana.*

Above: *The Case CC-4 was a convertible version of the row-crop CC, shown here with a wide front axle. To increase crop clearance, a spacer was used between the axle and radiator.*

Left: *Brochure for the Case Model C.*

Case Models R, RC, S, SC

In the mid-1930s, tractor manufacturers were filling the vacuum left by the departure of the popular Fordson with their own machines of under 20 hp. The John Deere B and Farmall F-12 were examples, and the RC row-crop tractor was introduced by Case as a competitor to these and others. The RC featured a side-valve four-cylinder engine from Waukesha rather than a Case-built engine. In 1938, the standard-tread R was added. In 1939, the R Series was updated with stylish new sheet metal and a cast iron "sunburst" grill. The paint, which had been a light gray, was now Flambeau Red.

Production of the R Series was stopped in favor of the new S Series in model year 1940. The S, a 1941 year model, was a smaller version of the D. It was available in a complete range of versions, but the S standard and the SC row-crop were the largest sellers. A new engine from Case powered the S Series. It was a short-stroke, high-speed powerplant that offered good power at a reasonable weight. In 1953, the bore was increased from 3.50 inches (87.5 mm) to 3.625 inches (90.625 mm). Gasoline was the standard fuel, but distillate was optional.

Models and Variations

Model	Years Built
R	1938–1940
RC	1935–1940
S	1941–1954
SC	1941–1954

Specifications: 1953 Case Model SC

Engine: Overhead-valve four-cylinder
Bore & stroke: 3.625x4.00 inches
(90.625x100 mm)
Displacement: 165 ci (2,703 cc)
Power: 30 belt hp
Transmission: Four speeds forward
Weight: 5,000 pounds (2,250 kg)

A 1938 styled row-crop Case RC. Characteristic of the RC was the "Chicken Roost" steering arm. Owner: Loren Engle of Abilene, Kansas. Engle's father bought this tractor new.

A 1937 Case RC. The RC was Case's answer to the Farmall F-12 and other small tractors. Case advertising warned that the RC was a supplement, not a replacement, for its larger tractors.

A 1939 standard-tread Case Model R. This was the first year for the styled Model R, sporting the attractive cast sunburst grill. This was also the first year for Flambeau Red paint.

Above, top: *Fred Bork was the original owner of this 1942 Case SC. Elwood J. Voss of Ashton, Illinois, is the second, and present, owner and restorer.*

Above, center: *An unstyled 1938 Case Model R, still in the lighter shade of gray. The Model R, as well as the RC, used a Waukesha L-head four-cylinder engine.*

Above, bottom: *The Case S was available with an adjustable wide front axle as shown here. This example also has some beefy wheel weights.*

Case Models V, VC, VAC, VAH, VAS

Former Case dealer Weston Rink of Ridgeland, Wisconsin, owns this pretty Case Model VAH. It is the high-clearance, but not offset, version of the basic Model VA. Only about 2,000 were made.

The V Series was introduced to appeal to the smaller-scale farmer. The horsepower of the S Series had increased, leaving the under-20-hp market again open, and the V stepped in to fill this niche. The V was assembled largely of vender-supplied components, including a Continental side-valve engine and gears supplied by Clark Equipment Company. The engine had enough power and the tractor enough weight that it overshadowed the more-expensive S in drawbar pull. This, plus the fact that the vender components were hurting profitability, led Case to redesign the unit in 1942 after just three production years. The new VA Series had Case-built components, but retained the same appearance as the V. The VA was the first to acquire the three-point Eagle Hitch in 1953.

A 1939 Case VC. The deeply flared rear fenders are characteristic of the early DC. Owner: Warren Kemper of Wapello, Iowa.

A rare 1941 Case VAS. Only 1,600 of this offset high-clearance cultivating tractor were built. Owner: J. R. Gyger of Lebanon, Indiana.

The Case Model VAO was a Model VA tractor with orchard sheet metal. This nicely restored 1947 model is owned by Dan Buckert of Hamilton, Illinois.

Models and Variations

Model	Years Built
V Standard-tread	1940–1942
VC Row-crop	1940–1942
VO Orchard	1941–1942
VA Standard-tread	1942–1953
VAC Dual-tricycle row-crop	1942–1953
VAC-11 Single front wheel	1951–1953
VAC-12 Dual-tricycle row-crop	1951–1953
VAC-13 Adj. Wide-front row-crop	1951–1953
VAC-14 Utility configuration	1953–1954
VAO Orchard	1942–1955
VAO-15 Orchard version of VAC-14	1953–1954
VAH High clearance	1947–1955
VAS Offset high clearance	1951–1954

Specifications: 1949 Case Model VAC

Engine: Overhead-valve four-cylinder
Bore & stroke: 3.25x3.75 inches (81.25x93.75 mm)
Displacement: 124 ci (2,031 cc)
Power: 20 belt hp (on gasoline)
Transmission: Four speeds forward
Weight: 3,200 pounds (1,440 kg)

Case Model 400

For the 1955 model year, the all-new Case 400, from the Racine works, replaced the D Series. It was available in gasoline, diesel, and LPG versions and in all of the various front-end configurations. The engine developed for the 400 was actually a four-cylinder version of the 500's six. The eight-speed transmission was a first for Case. In another departure from the past, the hand clutch (except for some specials) and the chain final drive were not used. The 400 was available both as a standard-tread and row-crop machine.

The Case Model 400 was available in a variety of styles, but the general-purpose type, as shown here in the single-front-wheel version, was by far the most popular. This is a 1955 model.

This 1956 Case Model 400 High Clearance is one of only 150 made; it came from the sugar cane fields of Louisiana. Owner: Jay Foxworthy.

Models and Variations		Specifications: Case 400
Model	Years Built	Engine: Overhead-valve four-cylinder
400 Diesel standard-tread	1955–1957	Bore & stroke: 4.00x4.00 inches
401 Diesel tricycle-front	1955–1957	(100x100 mm)
402 Diesel orchard	1955–1957	Displacement: 251 ci (4,111 cc)
403 Diesel high clearance	1955–1957	Power: 50 PTO hp
410 Gas standard-tread	1955–1957	Transmission: Eight speeds forward
420 LPG standard-tread	1955–1957	Weight: 6,600 pounds (2,970 kg)

Case Models 300 and 350

The Case Model 300 replaced the VA tractors on the Rock Island assembly lines in 1955. It was considerably more capable, however, and was a full three-bottom tractor. The Flambeau Red cast iron and Desert Sunset sheet metal was the same color scheme as that of the Racine-built 400, but the styling of the 300 was unique, especially its "sewer-grate" rear wheels. A Case-built engine of 148 ci (2,424-cc) displacement was available in gasoline, distillate, and LPG fuel versions. A Continental diesel of 157 ci (2,572 cc) was also offered. The basic transmission was a four-speed unit, while two- and three-range auxiliaries were optional. With the three-range auxiliary, twelve speeds forward and three reverse were provided.

The usual three-letter designators were used to denote engine type and front-end configuration. The first number of the three-number scheme indicated the number of plows the tractor was rated for; the second number indicated the fuel type; and the third number, the tractor's configuration, such as front-end type or orchard.

The tractor was upgraded in 1957 with spark-ignition engine displacement increased to 164 ci (2,868 cc); the designation was then changed to 350.

Models and Variations

Model	Years Built
300	1955–1957
350	1957–1958

Specifications: Case 301 Diesel

Engine: Overhead-valve four-cylinder
Bore & stroke: 3.375x4.375 inches (84.385x109.375 mm)
Displacement: 157 ci (2,572 cc)
Power: 30 belt hp
Transmission: Four, eight, or twelve speeds forward
Weight: 5,500 pounds (2,475 kg)

The Case Model 300 was built between 1955 and 1958. Although its heritage was clear, the 300 looked like it came from a different company than its stablemate, the Model 400.

Caterpillar Tractor Company
Peoria, Illinois, USA

Holt, Best, and Caterpillar Models 2-Ton, Ten, Fifteen, Flathead Twenty

Caterpillar was formed in 1925 by the merger of two industrial powerhouses: C. L. Best Tractor Company of San Leandro, California, and Holt Manufacturing Company of Stockton, California. Earlier, in 1908, Holt had taken over the Best Manufacturing Company, run by Daniel Best, father of C. L. Best. In 1910, Holt had registered the trade name "Caterpillar," which has since become virtually a generic name for crawlers.

Holt and both Best companies had been instrumental in the development of crawlers. After the 1925 merger, the new company established its headquarters in Peoria, Illinois. Holt brought its 2-Ton, 5-Ton, and 10-Ton models to the new company, whereas Best contributed its Model Thirty and Model Sixty. The 5-Ton and 10-Ton models were soon dropped, however.

Caterpillar's diminutive 2-Ton model was nearly identical to its predecessor, the Holt T35, and was powered by a four-cylinder, 251-ci (4,111-cc) gas engine. The Ten was the smallest Caterpillar ever made. It featured a 143-ci (2,342-cc), four-cylinder gas engine, and was available in standard, wide, and high versions. The Ten became the "Small" Fifteen (7C) in 1932 when many improvements were incorporated.

The "Big" Fifteen (PV) was an enlarged version of the Ten. It had a 220-ci (3,604-cc), side-valve engine. High and wide variations were available. The Twenty (8C) was the result of a 1932 re-rating of the "Big" Fifteen. It was called the Twenty Flathead, as it used the same 220-ci (3,604-cc), side-valve engine of the previous Fifteen, differentiating it from the older Twenty L and PL Series. The Twenty Flathead was one of the first Caterpillars to be painted Highway Yellow.

A beautifully restored Caterpillar Ten wide-track. Owner: Bob Hill of Manitoba, Canada. (Photograph by Bob LaVoie)

Above: *A pair of Caterpillar Fifteens. Owner: Keith Clark of Spokane, Washington. (Photograph by Bob LaVoie)*

Left: *A Caterpillar Ten fitted with plowing gear. (Photograph by Bob LaVoie)*

Models and Variations

Model	Years Built
2-Ton	1925–1928
Ten	1928–1933
"Big" Fifteen (PV)	1929–1932
"Small" Fifteen (7C)	1932–1933
Twenty Flathead (8C)	1932–1934

Specifications: Caterpillar Ten

Engine: L-head four-cylinder
Bore & stroke: 3.375x4.00 inches (84.375x100 mm)
Displacement: 143 ci (2,342 cc)
Power: 15 drawbar hp
Transmission: Three speeds forward
Weight: 4,330 pounds (1,949 kg)

Caterpillar Twenty, Twenty-Five, Twenty-Eight, R3, Twenty-Two, R2, D2

The Twenty L and PL Series was introduced in 1927. Not to be confused with the later Twenty Flathead, which was derived from the Cat Fifteen in 1932, this earlier Model Twenty had a 277-ci (4,537-cc), overhead-valve engine.

The Twenty-Five was merely a 1931 redesignation of the OHV Twenty reflecting its power capabilities. These left the factory in yellow livery. In 1933, the Twenty-Five was updated to the Twenty-Eight, sold in standard and wide-gauge widths, and in an orchard version. The Twenty-Eight retained the 277-ci (4,537-cc) engine.

The R3 was similar to the Twenty-Eight, but had its cylinders cast in pairs, rather than individually. Displacement was increased to 350 ci (5,733 cc) by increasing the bore, thus giving the tractor about 35 hp. Only about sixty R3s were made. The "R" designator is believed to indicate U.S. government–ordered models with peculiar specifications.

Introduced in 1934, the Twenty-Two was the most popular of the small Cats, with some 15,000 sold by 1939. It featured a 251-ci (4,111-cc), overhead-valve, four-cylinder engine. The R2 5E Series was a slight variation of the popular Twenty-Two. They were produced together for several years, but only eighty-three of the R2s were completed.

In 1938, the all-new R2 J Series was introduced with a 221-ci (3,620-cc) engine. This tractor had a five-speed gearbox, rather than the three speeds of the earlier 5E version.

In 1931, Caterpillar had pioneered the use of diesel engines, and the D2 of 1938 was the diesel version of the R2 J Series. The D2 also came in various series, the later ones using a larger, more powerful engine of 252 ci (4,128 cc), producing 42 belt hp.

Models and Variations	
Model	Years Built
Twenty	1927–1931
Twenty-Two	1934–1939
Twenty-Five	1931–1933
Twenty-Eight	1933–1935
R3	1934–1935
R2	1934–1942
D2	1938–1960

Specifications: 1952 Caterpillar D2
Engine: Overhead-valve four-cylinder
Bore & stroke: 4.00x5.00 inches
   (100x125 mm)
Displacement: 252 ci (4,128 cc)
Power: 29 drawbar hp, 42 belt hp
Transmission: Five speeds forward
Weight: 8,500 pounds (3,825 kg)

A Caterpillar Twenty-Five. Owner: Bob Hill of Manitoba, Canada. (Photograph by Bob LaVoie)

A Caterpillar Twenty-Eight. (Photograph by Bob LaVoie)

Caterpillar Thirty, R4, RD4, D4

The Thirty began life in 1921 as the Best 30. It continued as the Caterpillar Thirty (S) until 1930 with some 7,000 having been manufactured in the San Leandro, California, plant. Production of the Thirty (PS) continued in Peoria, Illinois, through 1932. It was available in both wide and narrow gauges. The four-cylinder engine displaced 461 ci (7,551 cc) and was coupled to a three-speed transmission.

The Thirty was redesigned and reintroduced in 1935 as the Thirty 6G Series. Also available in wide and narrow gauges, this tractor was renamed the R4 after 874 units were delivered. A four-cylinder, overhead-valve engine of 312 ci (5,111 cc) powered the Thirty G/R4. The RD4 was the diesel-powered version introduced in 1936, using the same engine block and five-speed transmission. After about 9,000 G Series tractors left the Peoria line, the R designator was dropped.

In 1947, the D4 U Series replaced the G. A 350-ci (5,733-cc) diesel engine replaced the old unit, making the D4 capable of 45 drawbar hp. Production of D4 variants continues to this day, although they currently are in the 80-hp category.

Models and Variations

Model	Years Built
Thirty S Series	1921–1932
Thirty G Series/R4	1935–1944
RD4/D4	1936–Present

Specifications:
Caterpillar Thirty G Series
Engine: Overhead-valve four-cylinder
Bore & stroke: 4.25x5.50 inches
  (106x137.5 mm)
Displacement: 312 ci (5,111 cc)
Power: 34 hp
Transmission: Five speeds forward
Weight: 10,000 pounds (4,500 kg)

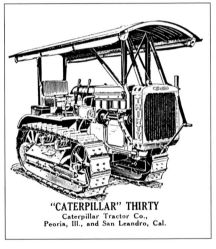

"CATERPILLAR" THIRTY
Caterpillar Tractor Co.,
Peoria, Ill., and San Leandro, Cal.

Above: *Caterpillar Thirty brochure illustration.*

Left: *A Caterpillar D4 fitted with armor plating advances with troops during the World War II Solomon Island campaign.*

Caterpillar Thirty-Five, Diesel Thirty-Five, Forty, Diesel Forty, R5, D5, RD6, R6, D6

When the Thirty PS was discontinued in 1932, the Thirty-Five was created to fill the gap. It was basically the same as the old Best Thirty but restyled to look like the rest of the Caterpillar line and powered by a larger, 485-ci (7,944-cc), four-cylinder engine. The diesel version arrived in 1933, with a three-cylinder engine of 520 ci (8,518 cc) and a four-speed transmission.

A 1934 Caterpillar Diesel Forty 55-hp tractor. The three-cylinder Diesel Forty became the RD6 in 1936 when designations on all Cats were changed.

In 1934, the Forty replaced the Thirty-Five. A 536-ci (8,780-cc), four-cylinder engine was used with a four-speed gearbox, and it was capable of 9,500 pounds (4,275 kg) of drawbar pull and weighed about 14,000 pounds (6,300 kg). The Diesel Forty used the Thirty-Five's three-cylinder engine, although the bore was increased at the end of the production run, upping displacement to 623 ci (10,205 cc). The Diesel Forty weighed 16,000 pounds (7,200 kg).

The R5 was produced with the Thirty-Five and Forty. The R5 models with the serial number prefix 5E were similar to the Thirty-Fives; the R5 with the 4H prefix was much like the Forty; and the R5 with the 3R prefix was the gas alternative to the diesel RD6.

In 1936, the Diesel Forty was redesignated the RD6 when the numbered series gave way to the R and RD designators. An R6 version was produced in 1941, but only one is known to exist; others were probably converted to the D6 configuration. Similarly, a D5 model was produced in limited numbers, and only three or four exist.

The all-new D6 came out in 1941, featuring a six-cylinder diesel of 468 ci (7,666 cc) and a five-speed transmission. In 1947, the U Series featured a 525-ci (8,600-cc) six-cylinder engine. The D6 is still in Caterpillar's lineup.

Models and Variations		Specifications: 1949 Caterpillar D6
Model	Years Built	Engine: Overhead-valve six-cylinder
Thirty-Five	1932–1934	Bore & stroke: 4.50x5.50 inches
Diesel Thirty-Five	1933–1934	(112.5x137.5 mm)
Forty	1934–1936	Displacement: 525 ci (8,600 cc)
Diesel Forty	1934–1936	Power: 69 hp
R5	1934–1940	Transmission: Five speeds forward
RD6	1936–1938	Weight: 19,000 pounds (8,550 kg)
D6	1941–Present	

Caterpillar Fifty, Diesel Fifty, Sixty, Diesel Sixty, Sixty-Five, Seventy

A 1931 Caterpillar Diesel Sixty. The Best Sixty became the Cat Sixty after the merger of 1925; this then became the Diesel Sixty when the new diesel engine was fitted in 1931.

Produced between 1931 and 1937, the Fifty was a big machine weighing more than 18,000 pounds (8,100 kg). It was the first Caterpillar to have a regular hood, rather than the full canopy. A four-cylinder, overhead-valve engine of 618 ci (10,123 cc) was used. The Diesel Fifty debuted in 1933 with a 693-ci (11,351-cc) engine. Both used four-speed gearboxes.

The Sixty began life as the Best Sixty. First introduced in 1919, it quickly built a reputation for reliability and work output, and was continued without much change after the merger forming Caterpillar. In 1931, it became the Caterpillar "Diesel," also known as the Diesel Sixty; to avoid confusion, the designation was changed to Diesel Sixty-Five. This was the first production diesel tractor and the first Caterpillar to be painted Highway Yellow. The gas Sixty-Five was a modernization of the original Sixty that extended its production life to 1933. It still used the crowbar starter, however.

Using the same gasoline 1,309-ci (21,441-cc), four-cylinder engine as the Sixty-Five, the Seventy got more power due to a 50-rpm increase in rated speed. It also had a four-speed transmission, rather than the three-speed unit of the Sixty-Five.

Models and Variations		Specifications:
Model	Years Built	1931 Caterpillar Diesel Sixty
Fifty	1931–1937	Engine: Overhead-valve four-cylinder
Diesel Fifty	1933–1936	Bore & stroke: 6.125x9.25 inches
Sixty	1919–1931	(153x231.25 mm)
Diesel Sixty/Sixty-Five	1931–1932	Displacement: 1,090 ci (17,854 cc)
Sixty-Five	1932–1933	Power: 77 belt hp
Seventy	1933–1937	Transmission: Three speeds forward
		Weight: 26,000 pounds (11,700 kg)

Caterpillar Diesel Seventy, Diesel Seventy-Five, D7, D8

When the gas Seventy was introduced in 1933, it was built on a new, modern chassis. To make the Diesel Seventy, the 1,090-ci (17,854-cc) engine from the Diesel Sixty-Five was installed with a six-speed gearbox.

Later that year, Caterpillar introduced a new engine design in three-, four-, and six-cylinder versions all using a bore and stroke of 5.25x8.00 inches (131.25x200 mm). The six-cylinder engine was fitted to the Diesel Seventy chassis; it became the Diesel Seventy-Five. It weighed 32,000 pounds (14,400 kg) and produced 93 belt hp.

For 1936, the numbered model names were replaced by R and RD designators; this system continued until 1938 when the RD became simply the now-famous D. Thus, the Diesel Seventy-Five became the RD8 and then the D8. The standard engine design had a bore increase to 5.75 inches (143.75 mm) in 1936.

The RD7 came out in 1936 using the four-cylinder version of the standard engine. It had a four-speed transmission and weighed 21,000 pounds (9,450 kg). Versions of the D7 and D8 are still in the Caterpillar line.

The six-cylinder engine of the Caterpillar Diesel Seventy-Five. The two-cylinder pony motor starter is on the other side. This starter motor used the same pistons as the little Cat Ten.

Models and Variations

Model	Years Built
Diesel Seventy	1933–1933
Diesel Seventy-Five	1933–1935
D7	1936–Present
D8	1936–Present

Specifications: 1936 Caterpillar RD8
Engine: Overhead-valve six-cylinder
Bore & stroke: 5.75x8.00 inches
    (143.75x200 mm)
Displacement: 1,246 ci (20,409 cc)
Power: 103 hp
Transmission: Six speeds forward
Weight: 34,000 pounds (15,300 kg)

A 1934 Caterpillar Diesel Seventy-Five, the forerunner of the famous D8. Carl Skirvin of Philomath, Oregon, is at the controls.

Cockshutt Farm Equipment Company

Brantford, Ontario, Canada

Cockshutt 30

The Canadian Cockshutt Plow Company was formed in 1877. Seeders, planters, disks, and other equipment were offered in addition to a full line of plows. Beginning in 1924, Cockshutt marketed Hart-Parr tractors with orange and yellow paint and the Cockshutt name cast into the radiator shell. A falling out occurred in 1928, and Cockshutt switched to tractors by Allis-Chalmers. By 1934, however, Cockshutt returned to the Oliver (Hart-Parr) line. This relationship continued to the end of World War II.

The Cockshutt 30 signified many firsts. It was the first proprietary tractor by Cockshutt, the first Canadian-built tractor tested at the University of Nebraska, and one of the first, if not the first, tractors to incorporate a live PTO. The engine was supplied by Buda. A four-speed transmission was incorporated, but a two-speed auxiliary was optional, giving eight speeds forward and two in reverse. Initially, only gasoline and distillate fuel versions were supplied, but in the 1950s, diesel and LPG engines were added. The customer had the choice of narrow or wide front ends.

The 30 was sold in the United States as the Co-op E3 by the National Farm Machinery Cooperative of Bellevue, Ohio, and as the Farmcrest, offered through the famous American Gambles Stores chain.

Models and Variations

Model	Years Built
30	1946–1956

Specifications: Cockshutt 30 gasoline

Engine: Overhead-valve four-cylinder
Bore & stroke: 3.44x4.13 inches (86x103.25 mm)
Displacement: 153 ci (2,506 cc)
Power: 30 hp
Transmission: Four speeds forward (eight forward and two reverse with optional underdrive)
Weight: 3,600 pounds (1,620 kg)

Advertisement for Cockshutt's 1956 lineup of eighteen different tractor models, including the venerable 30.

Cockshutt 40, 50, 35

The first of this series was the Cockshutt 40. Besides being somewhat larger than the 30, it was distinguished by its over-the-engine steering arrangement. The 40 used a Buda 230-ci (3,767-cc) six-cylinder engine in gasoline distillate and diesel versions. The transmission had six speeds forward and two in reverse; an auxiliary was not offered. Narrow and wide front ends were available. Live PTO and hydraulics were options. The 40 was sold in the United States as the Co-op E4.

The Cockshutt 50 and D-50 diesel were added to the line in 1953. They were the same as the 40, except the engine displacement was increased to 273 ci (4,472 cc) by omitting the cylinder sleeves. No distillate version of the 50 was offered. The 50 became the Co-op E5 in the United States.

In 1953, Cockshutt switched engines. The 40 was changed to a four-cylinder Perkins diesel of 269.5 ci (4,413 cc), and the designation was changed to 40D4 in Canada and to Golden Eagle in the United States. At the same time, the Hercules 198-ci (3,243-cc) engine was installed in the 40, and it was redesignated as the 35 (Canada) and Blackhawk 35 (United States). This tractor then replaced the 30 Series.

The Cockshutt 50 was the same as the Cockshutt 40, except for increased engine displacement and larger tires.

Models and Variations		Specifications: Cockshutt D-50
Model	Years Built	Engine: Overhead-valve six-cylinder
40	1949–1953	Bore & stroke: 3.75x4.13 inches
50, D-50	1953–1957	(93.75x103.25 mm)
40D4, Golden Eagle	1953–1957	Displacement: 273 ci (4,472 cc)
35, Blackhawk 35	1956–1957	Power: 52 PTO hp
		Transmission: Six speeds forward, two reverse
		Weight: 6,000 pounds (2,700 kg)

Essentially the same as the old Cockshutt 40, the Deluxe 35 used a Hercules powerplant, instead of the Buda. This 1956 model is owned by Jim Grant of Georgetown, Ontario.

Using a six-cylinder Buda engine, the Cockshutt 50 was a creditable 50-hp tractor. A 1954 diesel version is shown here at the Great Canadian Farm Field Days in Milton, Ontario.

Cockshutt 20

Also designated the Co-op E3 (replacing the former 30-based E3), the 20 began life in 1952 with a Continental L-head engine of 124 ci (2,031 cc) displacement. This proved to be inadequate, so before a full year of production, the bore was increased from 3.00 inches (75 mm) to 3.20 inches (80 mm), increasing displacement to 140 ci (2,293 cc). Both distillate and gasoline versions of the engine were available. The 20 was equipped with a four-speed transmission. Hydraulics and a live PTO were options. The diminutive Cockshutt 20 had a basic weight of only 2,800 pounds (1,260 kg), yet in its Nebraska test, it was able to pull 3,300 pounds (1,485 kg) in its maximum drawbar pull test. Of course some 1,600 pounds (720 kg) of ballast were added for the test.

A 1958 Cockshutt 20 Deluxe. Owner: Jim Grant of Georgetown, Ontario.

Models and Variations

Model	Years Built
20	1952–1958

Specifications: Cockshutt 20

Engine: Side-valve four-cylinder
Bore & stroke: 3.20x4.38 inches
 (80x109.5 mm)
Displacement: 140 ci (2,293 cc)
Power: 28 belt hp
Transmission: Four speeds forward
Weight: 2,800 pounds (1,260 kg)

Cockshutt 540, 550, 560, 570, 570 Super

The Cockshutt 80 began life as the Hart-Parr 18/28.

For the 1958 model year, the Cockshutt lineup of tractors was given a complete restyling by the famous industrial designer Raymond Loewy. The 540 (gasoline only) replaced the 20; the 550 (gas or diesel) replaced the 35; the 560 (diesel only) replaced the 40D4; and the 570 (gas or diesel) replaced the 50. All used six-speed transmissions without auxiliaries.

On February 1, 1962, the White Motor Company of Oak Brook, Illinois, purchased Cockshutt, and the name of the Canadian company was changed to the Cockshutt Farm Equipment Company of Canada, Ltd. White, which had also acquired Oliver and Minneapolis-Moline, assigned Canadian dealerships to Cockshutt and U.S. dealerships to Oliver/M-M. The Cockshutt plant in Brantford manufactured combines for the various sales organizations, while tractors were manufactured in Charles City, Iowa. Tractors from Charles City for Canada were Olivers, but were painted in Cockshutt colors and used the Cockshutt name. History has a way of repeating itself.

Models and Variations		Specifications:
Model	Years Built	Cockshutt 550 gasoline
540	1958–1962	Engine: Overhead-valve four-cylinder
550	1958–1961	Bore & stroke: 3.74x4.50 inches
560	1958–1961	(93.5x112.5 mm)
570	1958–1960	Displacement: 198 ci (3,243 cc)
570 Super	1961–1962	Power: 42 hp
		Transmission: Six speeds forward
		Weight: 5,700 pounds (2,565 kg)

Co-operative Manufacturing Company
Battle Creek, Michigan, USA

Co-op No. 1, No. 2, No. 3, B2JR

There have been several tractor manufacturers calling their products by the Co-op name, including Cockshutt. Some of the most interesting, however, were those presented by the Co-operative Manufacturing Company, which was also known as the Duplex Machinery Company.

The No. 1 was powered by a Waukesha four-cylinder engine, the No. 2 and No. 3 by 201-ci (3,292-cc) and 217-ci (3,554-cc) Chrysler industrial engines. Although being governed at 1,500 rpm limited the power of these tractors, the larger Chrysler engine was rated at 95 hp. Nevertheless, the Co-ops were among the fastest stock tractors, the No. 2 being capable of 28 mph (45 km/h).

In 1940, the marque was revived by the Arthurdale Farm Equipment Corporation of West Virginia, and the B2JR model was built through 1941.

Left: *A Co-op Duplex B2JR, an updated version of the No. 2. Owner: Fred Farms of Rochester, Indiana.*

Below: *A Co-op Duplex No. 2, powered by a Chrysler Industrial engine. Quite a number of these unusual tractors came from the Battle Creek, Michigan, factory in 1937 and 1938.*

Models and Variations

Model	Years Built
No. 1	1937–1938
No. 2	1937–1938
No. 3	1937–1938
B2JR	1940–1941

Specifications: Co-op No. 2

Engine: Side-valve six-cylinder
Displacement: 201 ci (3,292 cc)
Power: 33 hp
Transmission: Four speeds forward
Weight: 3,800 pounds (1,710 kg)

Deere & Company

Moline, Illinois, USA

Waterloo Boy Models R and N

Deere & Company's roots go back to 1837, when the firm was founded by blacksmith John Deere, who became a legend in his own time. Fame initially came to John Deere for the development of the self-scouring steel plow. He then built his firm into one of the country's most important implement manufacturers.

Tractors did not come as easily for Deere as for other makers of the time. Deere made several attempts to build a proprietary tractor, but none seemed to be the right machine at the right price. When the Waterloo Gasoline Engine Company of Waterloo, Iowa, came up for sale, Deere bought it in 1918, and continued to produce its successful Waterloo Boy tractor until 1924.

The Waterloo Boy company, and then Deere, produced the Model R from 1915 to 1919. It was a four-wheel, rear-wheel-drive machine with one forward and one reverse speed. The engine was a horizontal side-by-side, two-cylinder of 333 ci (5,455 cc) displacement; this type of engine would characterize Deere tractors for the next forty-two years. Displacement was increased to 395 ci (6,470 cc) in 1915, and to 465 ci (7, 617 cc) in 1917.

Model N production overlapped the R beginning in 1917 and continuing to 1924. The N had a two-speed transmission, and other improvements were added over time. The N can be identified by the main drive gear, which is almost the same diameter as the wheel; on the R, this gear is about half of the diameter of the rim.

Models and Variations	
Model	Years Built
R	1915–1918
N	1917–1924

Specifications: Waterloo Boy N
Engine: Overhead-valve two-cylinder
Bore & stroke: 6.50x7.00 inches
    (162.5x175 mm)
Displacement: 465 ci (7,617 cc)
Power: 25 belt hp
Transmission: Two speeds forward
Weight: 6,300 pounds (2,835 kg)

Advertisement for John Deere's Waterloo Boy 12/25:
"Experience has demonstrated that this three-plow trac-
tor, with 25 H.P. at belt is the ideal 'general utility'
tractor for any size farm."

A 1920 Waterloo Boy Model N. John Deere took over the Waterloo Boy outfit in 1918 and kept them in production through 1924. Owner: Don Wolf of Fort Wayne, Indiana.

A beautifully restored Waterloo Boy Model R. (Photograph courtesy John Deere)

John Deere Model D

A John Deere Model D. (Photograph by Robert N. Pripps)

Overlapping production of the Waterloo Boy, the first two-cylinder tractor to bear the John Deere name was the famous and venerable Model D. The D holds the record for longest production run of any American tractor at thirty years, during which time some 160,000 were delivered.

When Deere took over the Waterloo Boy outfit in 1918, the Waterloo Boy engineers were working on a new design. Deere continued development through four prototypes, each given a letter designator A through D. The D version became the Model D. Conventional tractor layout in the 1923–1924 period was adopted for the D; therefore, it did not resemble the Waterloo Boy in appearance, but under the skin the D retained the Waterloo Boy's characteristics. It used a two-speed transmission up to 1935. The side-by-side horizontal two-cylinder engine was increased in displacement from 465 to 501 ci (7,617 to 8,206 cc) at serial number 53383 in 1927. The steering wheel was moved from the left side to the right for improved plowing visibility in 1931 at number 109944. Styled sheet metal penned by famous industrial designer Henry Dreyfuss was added in 1939 at number 143800. Power rose from 30 belt hp in 1923 to 42 in 1953.

Models and Variations

Model	Years Built	Serial Numbers	Remarks
D	1923–1924	30401–30450	26-inch (65-cm) spoked flywheel; welded front axle; ladder-side radiator
D	1924	31451–31279	Cast front axle
D	1924–1926	31280–36248	24-inch (60-cm) spoked flywheel
D	1926–1927	36249–53387	Solid flywheel
D	1927–1930	53388–109943	501-ci (8,206-cc) engine
D	1931–1934	109944–119099	Right-hand steering
D	1935–1938	119945–143799	Three-speed transmission
D	1939–1953	143800–191578	Styled

Specifications: 1953 John Deere Model D

Engine: Overhead-valve two-cylinder
Bore & stroke: 6.75x7.00 inches (168.75x175 mm)
Displacement: 501 ci (8,206 cc)
Power: 42 belt hp
Transmission: Three speeds forward
Weight: 5,300 pounds (2,385 kg)

Above: *The John Deere Model D was produced without many changes for thirty years, and more than 160,000 were built. Belt horsepower rose from 30 to 42 during the production run.*

Left: *Advertisement for John Deere's Model D: "It's More than a Success—It's a Real Sensation."*

It's More than a Success—It's a Real Sensation

That's the verdict coming from all over the country, wherever the John Deere Tractor is at work. Users get enthusiastic over its performance; neighbors join in—there's a real welcome for the

John Deere Tractor

HERE ARE THE REASONS:

Abundance of power to do all belt and drawbar work easily, rapidly and profitably.

Simpler by hundreds of parts, lighter by hundreds of pounds—a 15-27 tractor that weighs only 4,000 pounds—it does not pack the soil or mire down. Low and compact, it turns short and operates easily in close quarters.

Fewer and sturdier parts— made over-size—of the finest materials and workmanship.

Complete enclosure of working parts in a dust-proof, oil-tight case, thoroughly lubricated by

a simple, positive oiling system.

Most efficient final drive ever designed for tractors. Double-roller chain of hardened steel, completely enclosed and running in oil bath. Ideal for saving power, and outlasts this long-lived tractor.

All adjustments and repairs can be made easily and quickly by the operator, in a standing position.

Low initial cost, fuel and oil economy, faster working speeds, low upkeep cost and long life make it a safe, money-making investment for the farmer.

Above: *The John Deere Model R was Deere's first diesel-powered tractor. The Wheatland R was only available as a standard-tread machine. A 24.6-ci (403-cc) gasoline starter motor was used.*

Left: *The ultimate two-cylinder John Deere is the mighty Model 830, which was built only as a standard, or wheatland, machine. Owner: Don Wolf of Fort Wayne, Indiana.*

John Deere Models R, 80, 820, 830

With this series, Deere got into the diesel engine business. It was a good start, as Deere to this day is one of the foremost makers of diesels. The R of 1949 was expected to replace the Model D, but unexpectedly strong sales of the D postponed its demise until 1953; fuel consumption of the large, low-compression engines eventually forced the conversion to diesel by farmers.

The tractors of this series were all standard-treads, or wheatlands, primarily intended to pull multi-bottom plows. The first upgrade of the R came in 1955 with the change to the 80. The displacement was increased from 416 to 472 ci (6,814 to 7,731 cc), and the transmission was changed from a five- to a six-speed.

In 1956, two-tone sheet metal was added and the designation changed to 820. The same size engine was used, but power was increased 10 percent. Draft-control hydraulics were added. Then in 1958, the designation was changed to 830. It was improved in operator comfort and convenience, and now offered direct electric starting, in addition to the pony-motor option.

Models and Variations

Model	Years Built
R	1949–1954
80	1955–1956
820	1957–1958
830	1958–1960

Specifications: Deere Model 80

Engine: Overhead-valve two-cylinder
Bore & stroke: 6.125x8.00 inches (153x200 mm)
Displacement: 472 ci (7,731 cc)
Power: 68 PTO hp
Transmission: Six speeds forward
Weight: 7,850 pounds (3,533 kg)

John Deere Model R brochure.

John Deere Models A, 60, 620, 630

The year 1934 was a watershed year for John Deere, with the introduction of the John Deere A. Shown here is a Model AW (Wide) of 1935 vintage. Almost 300,000 Model As were sold during the tractor's production life.

The Model A of 1934 marked Deere's entry into the general-purpose market. Deere's Model GP disappointed Deere management in its competition with International Harvester. The A, therefore, was primarily a tricycle tractor, although, in true Deere fashion, all conceivable configurations were offered, including the AR standard-tread, AO orchard and later AOS streamlined orchard, AN single-front and AW adjustable wide-front, ANH and AWH high-crop, and AI industrial. The A received the Dreyfuss styling treatment in 1938.

In 1952, Deere changed from letter designators to two numbers. The A became the 60, with engine improvements giving a 10 percent power increase. Besides distillate and gasoline fuels, LPG was now offered. The 60 also offered live hydraulics and PTO.

The 620 came in 1956 with the draft-control three-point hitch called Custom-Powr-Trol. A 20 percent power increase came mostly through an increase in engine rpm from 975 to 1,125. The 630 was the last of the line, debuting in 1958. Power was the same, but improvements in operator convenience and a new four-light headlight system meant increased productivity. More than 70 percent of the 620s and 630s were narrow-fronts, but all the variations offered for the A were maintained. The distillate and LPG versions are rare now, but were offered throughout the life of the series.

Models and Variations

Model	Years Built
A	1934–1952
60	1952–1956
620	1956–1958
630	1958–1960

Specifications:
John Deere Model 620 row-crop

Engine: Overhead-valve two-cylinder
Bore & stroke: 5.50x6.75 inches
  (137.5x168.75 mm)
Displacement: 321 ci (10,172 cc)
Power: 48 hp (gasoline)
Transmission: Six speeds forward
Weight: 5,900 pounds (2,655 kg)

Left, top: *In 1938, the Model A John Deere tractor received the Dreyfuss styling treatment. In 1947, the frame was changed to this pressed-steel version. This 1949 model is an AWH with 12.4x42-inch (31x105-cm) rear tires.*

Left, bottom: *A 1946 John Deere Model AO (Orchard). This version of the Model A was based on the standard-tread AR with modifications made to allow the AO to slide under low-hanging branches.*

Below: *This 1938 John Deere Model ANH (Narrow High) is one of only twenty-six made. Owner: the Kellor family of Forest Junction, Wisconsin.*

Above: *The standard-tread John Deere Model AR. This one, a 1950 model, is owned by Jon Davis of Maplewood, Ohio, who inherited it from the original owner, his grand-father.*

Right, top: *A John Deere Hi-Crop Model 60. The Hi-Crop version was about 12 inches (30 cm) higher than the normal Model 60. A special drop-box drives the rear wheels; longer kingpins raise the front.*

Right, bottom: *A streamlined John Deere Model 60 Orchard on show. (Photograph by Robert N. Pripps)*

John Deere Models C and GP

The Model C was introduced in 1928 as Deere's answer to the Farmall general-purpose tractor. After just 110 units were delivered, confusion between the C and D designations led Deere to rename the C as the Model GP, for General Purpose. The GP was unique in that it was designed to be a three-row, rather than two-row, tractor. This explained its wide front end with an arched front axle to straddle the center row. The GP was also unique among Deere tractors in that it was the only horizontal Deere two-cylinder engine to use the L-head configuration. The GP featured a mechanical implement lift.

There were several variations on the GP theme: the tricycle GPWT wide tread, tricycle GP-P with long rear axles to straddle potato rows, and the wide-front GPO orchard version.

This may look like a John Deere GP, but it's a Model C that escaped the recall of 1928. Those recalled were renumbered, beginning with serial number 200111.

Models and Variations

Model	Years Built	Serial Numbers	Remarks
C	1928–1928	200111-200202	312 ci (5,111 cc)
GP	1928–1930	200211-223802	
GP	1930–1935	223803-230745	339 ci (5,553 cc)
GPWT	1929–1930	400000-405252	Wide tread
GP-P	1930	5000-5202	Potato tread
GPO	1931–1935	15000-15732	Orchard

Specifications: John Deere Model C/GP

Engine: Side-valve two-cylinder
Bore & stroke: 5.75x6.00 inches (143.75x150 mm) early;
    6.00x6.00 inches (150x150 mm) late
Displacement: 312 ci (5,111 cc) early; 339 ci (5,553 cc) late
Power: 20 belt hp
Transmission: Three speeds forward
Weight: 3,600 pounds (1,620 kg)

The John Deere Model GP was unique among John Deere tractors in that it used an L-head valve arrangement, rather than overhead valves, for its side-by-side two-cylinder engine.

The John Deere Model GPWT, or GP Wide-Tread, had long axles to allow it to straddle two rows. Originally, the steering shaft ran alongside the engine; in 1932, the shaft was repositioned over the engine. This is a 1933 model.

John Deere Models B, 50, 520, 530

A 1935 John Deere BW (Wide) on factory round-spoke wheels and rubber tires.

The Model B was the most popular of Deere's two-cylinder line, with more than 300,000 delivered. It was designed to be a smaller, cheaper running mate to the A, boasting all the features of the A. These included a hydraulic lift option, adjustable wheel tread, and all the various front-end configurations. The B was also available in standard-tread BR and orchard BO versions, as well as the BN single-front and BW wide-front, the BNH and BWH high-crop, and the BI industrial; the BO orchard crawler version was a modification by the Lindeman Brothers of Yakima, Washington.

The two-number series John Deere tractors came out in 1952 as a marketing ploy to give the line a modern image. Nifty, fresh sheet-metal styling by Henry Dreyfuss certainly accomplished that, but there were performance improvements, too. The engine was the same, but internal improvements gave 10 percent more power. Live hydraulics and PTO were added, as was an optional three-point lift. For the 520, a draft-control three-point hitch was included, and engine speed was upped from 1,250 to 1,325 rpm to increase power. The 530 incorporated improved ergonomics. All of the tractors in this series were available in distillate, LPG, and gasoline versions.

Models and Variations

Model	Years Built	Serial Numbers	Remarks
B	1935–1938	1000–59999	Unstyled; four-speed; 149 ci (2,441 cc)
B	1938–1940	60000–95999	Styled; 175 ci (2,867 cc)
B	1941–1947	96000–200999	Six-speed
B	1947–1952	201000–310775	Pressed-steel frame; 190 ci (3,112 cc)
50	1952–1956	5000001–5033751	
520	1956–1958	5200000–5213189	
530	1958–1960	5300000–5309814	

Specifications: John Deere Model 530

Engine: Overhead-valve four-cylinder
Bore & stroke: 4.69x5.50 inches (117.25x137.5 mm)
Displacement: 190 ci (3,122 cc)
Power: 39 belt hp
Transmission: Six speeds forward
Weight: 5,000 pounds (2,250 kg)

Above, top: *The John Deere Model BWH was wider and higher than the standard Model B. The one shown was built in 1938. Owner: the Kellor family of Forest Junction, Wisconsin.*

Above, center: *A 1941 John Deere Model B row-crop with the optional round-top fenders. The Models B and A look quite a bit alike, but generally, the tall exhaust stack identifies the Model B.*

Above, bottom: *The John Deere Model 520 replaced the Model 50 in 1956, which in turn was a descendant of the famous Model B.*

Above: *The John Deere Model B row-crop was introduced in 1935. Shortly thereafter, the standard-tread Model BR was added to the lineup. Shown is a 1935 Model BR.*

Left: *A 1958 John Deere 530 single-front-wheel row-crop. The 30 Series tractors incorporated ergonomic and safety improvements. Owner: Lyle Pals of Egan, Illinois.*

The John Deere Model GH Hi-Crop was made for working in tall crops, such as corn or cane. This nicely restored example is a 1953 model.

An extremely rare and beautifully restored John Deere 70 Hi-Crop LP, of which only twenty-five were made. The Model 70 replaced the Model G in 1953.

John Deere Models G, 70, 720, 730

The mighty G began life as a big brother to the successful Models A and B. It filled the niche for the farmer with a larger acreage and a larger thresher. The G came out in 1937 as a 1938 model just as optimism for the end of the Depression was on the increase. It was available in high-crop GH and single-front-wheel GN versions, but not as a standard-tread; that job was filled by the D. The G can be distinguished from the A by the bulge in the frame rails dictated by the G's broad engine.

The G became the Model 70 in 1953 with the change to the two-number system. The 70 was originally offered in distillate, gasoline, or LPG versions, but in 1954, a diesel was added. All versions were more powerful than the G. The 70 also offered live hydraulics and PTO. The 70 was available in various configurations, including a standard-tread version.

The Model 720 was an upgrade of the 70 offering Custom Powr-Trol, Deere's adaptation of Harry Ferguson's draft-control three-point hitch. The same fuel options were available, but the non-diesel engines were smaller in displacement and faster turning. As with the others in the Deere lineup, the improvements between the 720 and the 730 of 1958 were in the areas of operator convenience, safety, and comfort. A 24-volt starter was an option instead of the V-4 pony motor.

The last of the great line of two-cylinder row-crop tractors made by John Deere, the Model 730. Owner: Orv Rothgarn of Owatona, Minnesota.

Models and Variations

Model	Years Built
G	1938–1953
70	1953–1956
720	1956–1958
730	1958–1960

Specifications:
John Deere 730S Diesel

Engine: Overhead-valve two-cylinder
Bore & stroke: 6.12x6.40 inches (153x160 mm)
Displacement: 376 ci (6,159 cc)
Power: 59 PTO hp
Transmission: Six speeds forward
Weight: 7,800 pounds (3,510 kg)

Above: *This John Deere Model 720 Standard LP is part of the 20 Series introduced in 1956 and continued through 1958. It was capable of 60 belt hp.*

Left, top: *A 1959 John Deere Model 730 Diesel. The 30 Series replaced the 20 Series in 1958. It was produced into 1961, longer than the rest of the two-cylinder line.*

Left, bottom: *A 1953 John Deere Model GW.*

John Deere Model H

John Deere's Model H was a small tractor that met the needs of the small farmer at an affordable price. Owner: J. H. Chard of Axbridge, Great Britain.

The Model H came out in 1939 as a small row-crop tractor at a price a small-scale farmer could afford. Farmers with larger spreads found the H useful for smaller jobs. It was available in the normal dual narrow-front, as the single-front-wheel HN, the high-crop wide-front HWH, or as the single-front-wheel high-crop HNH.

The engine of the H was the traditional Deere horizontal side-by-side two-banger. As it was small, it needed to turn faster than the others, and rated speed was 1,400 rpm, but there was a governor override foot throttle that could schedule speeds up to 1,800 rpm.

An unusual feature of the H, due to the fast engine speed, was that power was taken from the end of the camshaft, rather than the crankshaft. With this, a 2:1 speed reduction was made. This meant simpler gearing downstream, elimination of the bull gears, brakes on the axleshafts, and a larger, slower belt pulley. The Model H was configured for distillate fuel.

Models and Variations		Specifications: John Deere Model H
Model	Years Built	Engine: Overhead-valve two-cylinder
H	1939–1947	Bore & stroke: 3.56x5.00 inches
HN	1939–1947	(89x125 mm)
HWH	1941–1942	Displacement: 90.7 ci (1,486 cc)
HNH	1941–1942	Power: 15 belt hp
		Transmission: Three speeds forward
		Weight: 3,000 pounds (1,350 kg)

A John Deere Model H with a mounted cultivator and sun umbrella. The little H was an economical tractor to use for cultivating chores.

John Deere Models 62, L, LA

A John Deere Model L. (Photograph by Robert N. Pripps)

The first of a new crop of lightweight tractors in the mid-1930s, this series originated with the John Deere Dubuque Wagon Works, rather than the Waterloo Tractor operation. The intention was that this line begin with a clean sheet of paper; the only stipulation was a two-cylinder engine be used.

The engineers began with a two-cylinder Novo engine and a Model A Ford car transmission (and steering wheel) to make the Model Y prototype. This was refined into the Model 62 with a Deere transmission and Hercules engine. Some seventy-eight of these production prototypes were sold to the public. For the 1937–1938 model year, the production Model L with a Hercules engine was sold in large quantities as an inexpensive replacement for a horse team. In late 1938, the L received the Dreyfuss styling touch. Starting in 1941, the more powerful and heavier LA, with its own serial number series, was added to the line, and produced simultaneously with the L. The L, from serial 625000 and on, as well as the LA, used a Deere-built engine.

These were the first John Deere two-cylinders to use a vertical engine, a foot clutch, and to employ a driveshaft. They were gasoline only. Besides the Model GP, they were the only Deeres to use an L-head engine.

Models and Variations

Model	Years Built	Serial Numbers	Remarks
62	1937-1937	621000-621078	57 ci (934 cc)
L	1937-1938	621079-622580	Unstyled
L, LI	1938-1941	625000-634840	Styled; 66 ci (1,081 cc)
LI	1942-1946	50001-52019	Late industrial
LA	1941-1946	1001-13475	76 ci (1,245 cc)

Specifications: John Deere Model LA

Engine: Side-valve two-cylinder
Bore & stroke: 3.50x4.00 inches (87.5x100 mm)
Displacement: 76 ci (1,245 cc)
Power: 14 hp
Transmission: Three speeds forward
Weight: 2,200 pounds (990 kg)

John Deere Models M, 40, 320, 330

A John Deere Model 40.

The Model M arrived after World War II as a replacement for the LA and H, and to counter the onslaught of the Ford-Ferguson. It was designed from the outset as a utility tractor, like the Ford, but soon Deere responded to customer demand for a row-crop version, and the Model MT was born. Like the LA, the M used a vertical two-cylinder engine, foot clutch, and driveshaft. It also had a hydraulic three-point implement lift, but not draft-control, as Deere was wary of Ferguson's patents. Next came the MC crawler, Deere having bought out the Lindeman Brothers, who had been converting Model Bs to tracks.

With the switch to the two-number system in 1953, the M became the 40. There were many improvements made to the 40, which came in seven different configurations, including a crawler and a high-crop. It boasted about 15 percent more power than the M on gasoline, and a distillate version was also offered.

The next variation was the 320, which used the same engine as the 40. It came in the standard and utility versions. There were, however, some factory-made special versions as well. The 320 was available with draft-control hydraulics, as Ford and Ferguson had battled out the patent situation by then. The 330 was the same as the 320, but with improvements in operator comfort and convenience.

Models and Variations		Specifications: John Deere Model M gasoline
Model	Years Built	Engine: Overhead-valve two-cylinder
M	1947–1952	Bore & stroke: 4.00x4.00 inches
MT	1949–1952	(100x100 mm)
MC	1949–1952	Displacement: 100.5 ci (1,646 cc)
40	1953–1955	Power: 21 PTO hp
320	1956–1958	Transmission: Four speeds forward
330	1958–1960	Weight: 2,550 pounds (1,148 kg)

The John Deere Model 320 was the successor to the Model 40. It included the Ferguson-type three-point hitch. This later version had the angled, rather than the vertical, steering wheel.

John Deere Models 420, 430, 435

The Model 420 was much the same as the 320. The big difference was increased displacement by increasing the engine bore, giving about a 20 percent power advantage. It was available in eight configurations, including the crawler, row-crop, high-crop, standard, utility, two-row utility, and two specials. Gasoline and distillate engines were available for all versions; LPG fuel was offered for all but the crawler.

The 430 featured a new slanted dash and steering wheel, along with other improvements to aid the operator in getting the most from the machine. An option on the 430 was a direction-reversing shifter. This was an advantage for tractors with loaders, allowing forward or reverse travel in any gear.

The 435 deferred to an engine made outside of Deere; it used a unique two-cylinder, two-cycle GM supercharged diesel. The tractor was otherwise the same as the 430, except for larger tires. The 435 was only produced in the model years 1959 and 1960. It was the first John Deere to offer the 1,000-rpm PTO.

Models and Variations	
Model	Years Built
420	1956–1958
430	1958–1960
435	1959–1960

Specifications:
John Deere Model 420T distillate
Engine: Overhead-valve two-cylinder
Bore & stroke: 4.25x4.00 inches
 (106.25x100 mm)
Displacement: 113.5 ci (1,859 cc)
Power: 23.5 PTO hp
Transmission: Four or five speeds forward
Weight: 3,000 pounds (1,350 kg)

Above, top: *The John Deere Model 420 was offered in a variety of tricycle- and wide-front styles.*

Above, center: *The John Deere 430 was sold in seven versions: 430W Row-Crop Utility (shown), 430U Utility, 430S Standard, 430H Hi-Crop, 430V Special, 430C Crawler, and the 430T Convertible.*

Above, bottom: *The John Deere Model 435 is basically a 430 Row-Crop Utility with a General Motors two-cylinder, two-cycle diesel engine. The 435 was made only in the last part of 1959 and 1960.*

Eagle Manufacturing Company

Appleton, Wisconsin, USA

Eagle Models E, F, H, 6A, 6B, 6C

One of the real pioneers of the tractor industry was the little-known Eagle Manufacturing Company. The company was formed in 1888 to manufacture farm engines and silo fillers, and made its first tractor in 1906, a 32-hp outfit with a two-cylinder engine and evaporative cooling. Various others of similar configuration but different sizes were later made. In about 1921, the Model E was introduced as a three-/four-plow machine with a two-cylinder horizontal engine with water pump, fan, and radiator cooling.

The Model F was variously rated as a 12/22 or 16/30 tractor. The H featured a massive 8.00x8.00-inch (200x200-mm) engine and was rated by the company as a 20/40, but the University of Nebraska rating was 16/30. These models were built into the mid-1930s, by which time they were antiquated designs. It is not known how many were sold.

In fall 1930, Eagle announced a more modern tractor design, the 6A, with a six-cylinder Hercules L-head engine. This was followed in 1936 by the 6B tricycle row-crop with a smaller Hercules six. The 6C was a standard-tread version of the 6B. Eagle sold out to the FWD Company of Wisconsin in 1940, and its tractors were discontinued.

Models and Variations

Model	Years Built
E	1921–1935
F	1922–1928
H	1921–1932
6A	1931–1938
6B	1936–1940
6C	1938–1940

Specifications: Eagle Model 6A

Engine: Side-valve six-cylinder
Bore & stroke: 4.00x4.75 inches
(100x118.75 mm)
Displacement: 358 ci (5,864 cc)
Power: 40 belt hp
Transmission: Three speeds forward
Weight: 5,700 pounds (2,565 kg)

A 1938 Eagle 6C. The 6C (standard) and the 6B (row-crop) had less power than the original 6A. All versions used Hercules engines.

The two-cylinder Eagle Model E was built between 1921 and 1935 in Appleton, Wisconsin.

Emerson-Brantingham Implement Company
Rockford, Illinois, USA

Big 4 and Reeves

Emerson-Brantingham was an outgrowth of the Manny Reaper Company, a firm that challenged Cyrus McCormick's patents (with the help of a young lawyer named Abraham Lincoln). Ralph Emerson, a cousin of poet Ralph Waldo Emerson, bought into the business and helped to expand it into a large farm equipment enterprise. Emerson brought Charles Brantingham into the firm, and he soon became president of the company renamed Emerson-Brantingham.

In 1912, E-B bought several companies to round out its lines, including Reeves & Company of Columbus, Indiana, and Gas Traction Company of Minneapolis, Minnesota. Both were manufacturing tractors that were continued under E-B. Reeves produced a giant 40/65 at the time of the E-B takeover using a four-cylinder engine of a whopping 1,486 ci (24,341 cc) mounted transverse to the line of travel. Gas Traction's famous Big 4 30/60 was a 21,000-pound (9,450-kg) four-cylinder, four-wheel mammoth with 8-foot (240-cm) wheels. A 20/35 model followed with a weight of only 10,000 pounds (4,500 kg); it was otherwise similar to the 30/60, but smaller. Like other tractor makers of the time, E-B took a flyer in the huge-tractor segment with a 45/90.

Models and Variations

Model	Years Built
Big 4 30/60	1912–1916
Big 4 20/35	1913–1919
Big 4 45/90	1913–1916
Reeves 45/60	1914–1920

Specifications:
Emerson-Brantingham 20/35
Engine: Side-valve four-cylinder
Bore & stroke: 5.00x7.00 inches (125x175 mm)
Displacement: 550 ci (9,009 cc)
Power: 35 hp
Transmission: One speed forward
Weight: 9,800 pounds (4,410 kg)

Advertisement for the Gas Traction Company's Big 4 Thirty: "The Modern Farm Power."

The Modern Farm Power

The Big Four "30" winning the Gold Medal in the World's Motor Competition at Winnipeg, 1911, pulling eight breaker bottoms in tough prairie sod on two gallons of fuel to the acre using no water. The Big Four "30" won Gold and Silver Medals in gasoline and kerosene classes, and excelled its wonderful, record-smashing performance of 1910, when it also won the Gold Medal.

With the Big Four "30" you can do your work better, quicker and cheaper than you are doing it with horses. It does the work of thirty first-class, fresh-to-the-minute draft horses and when it is not working it costs you not one penny. It never tires, never heats, never quits, but just eats up work, day after day, month after month and year after year.

Write Today for "The Book of Gas Traction Engines." It tells all about the modern way of farming by power. A postcard will bring the book.

Gas Traction Company
First and Largest Builder of Four-Cylinder Farm Tractors in the World
2703 University Ave. S. E.   MINNEAPOLIS, MINN.

Emerson-Brantingham Models L 12/20, Q 12/20, 9/16, AA 12/20, 20/35, 16/32

The Emerson-Brantingham Model Q 12/20 carried a four-cylinder engine of 354 ci (5,799 cc). The same engine was used in the Model AA 12/20.

Emerson-Brantingham prospered in Rockford, Illinois, becoming for a time the largest agricultural equipment manufacturer in the world. It built the largest manufacturing facility in the world—almost 200 acres (80 hectares) under roof. In 1916, the firm saw the trend to smaller, lighter tractors and brought out its first proprietary tractor, the three-wheel Model L 12/20, weighing only 5,500 pounds (2,475 kg). An improved Model Q 12/20 followed in 1917, using a 354-ci (5,799-cc) E-B engine; it was a four-wheel machine weighing 6,500 pounds (2,925 kg). Also in 1917, a smaller, 9/16 four-wheel tractor was presented. When the Fordson became available to North American farmers in 1918, E-B was aware that the 9/16 was not competitive, and so, in 1918, the Model AA 12/20 was ushered in. It used the same engine as the Model Q, but weighed only 4,400 pounds (1,980 kg).

An improved version of the Big-4 Model 20 20/35 was introduced in 1919 as the E-B 20/35. It used a side-valve four-cylinder engine of 550 ci (9,009 ci) and achieved its rating on gasoline. This machine was again modernized in 1921 with an increased bore diameter providing 606 ci (9,926 cc) and 16/32 hp on kerosene fuel. These tractors still used chain-and-windlass steering.

E-B was bought out by Case in 1928.

Models and Variations		Specifications: Emerson-Brantingham Model AA 12/20
Model	Years Built	
L 12/20	1916–1917	Engine: Side-valve four-cylinder
Q 12/20	1917–1928	Bore & stroke: 4.75x5.00 inches
9/16	1917–1920	(118.75x125 mm)
AA 12/20	1918–1928	Displacement: 354 ci (5,798 cc)
20/35	1919–1920	Power: 12 drawbar hp, 20 belt hp
16/32	1921–1928	Transmission: One speed forward
		Weight: 4,400 pounds (1,980 kg)

Emerson-Brantinghams were made in Rockford, Illinois. Shown is the Model Q 12/20 tractor that debuted in 1917. This four-wheel design replaced the similar three-wheel Model L.

Fate-Root-Heath Company
Plymouth, Ohio, USA

Plymouth, Silver King

A 1939 Model R-38 Silver King. Made by the Fate-Root-Heath Company of Plymouth, Ohio, the R-38 was originally called the Plymouth. The name was changed in 1935 to avoid conflict with Chrysler.

Fate-Root-Heath was a railroad locomotive builder founded in 1884. Its first tractor was the conventional Plymouth of 1933. It was equipped with a Hercules 3.00x4.00-in (75x100-mm) four-cylinder engine. One of its advertising claims was a 25-mph (40-km/h) transport speed. For the 1935 model year, it was renamed the Silver King R-38. From 1937 to 1939, a row-crop Silver King R-66 was added to the line. It employed a single front wheel and bull gears on the ends of the rear axles to gain crop clearance. The Hercules engine of the R-38 was retained, but the bore was increased to 3.25 inches (81.25 mm).

For 1940, the line was given a facelift and row-crop model numbers that reflected rear wheel spacing, the first two digits being the tread width in inches. The models were the 600, 660, and 720. The Silver King line was now powered by Continental-built 162-ci (2,654-cc) L-head engines. The line was again restyled for the 1945 model year with models identified as the 345 (single-front-wheel row-crop) and the 445 (standard-tread four-wheel). Model numbers indicated the number of wheels and the year model. This arrangement continued to 1953.

In 1955, the Silver King line was taken over by Mountain State Fabricating Company of Clarksburg, West Virginia. Model numbers were simply 370 (row-crop) and 371 (standard). Production ended in 1956.

Models and Variations		Specifications: Silver King R-66
Model	Years Built	Engine: Side-valve four-cylinder
R-38	1933–1939	Bore & stroke: 3.25x4.00 inches
R-66	1936–1939	(81.25x100 mm)
600, 660, 720	1940–1944	Displacement: 133 ci (2,178 cc)
345, 445-353, 453	1945–1953	Power: 20 hp
370, 371	1955–1956	Transmission: Four speeds forward
		Weight: 2,400 pounds (1,080 kg)

Harry Ferguson, Inc.

Detroit, Michigan, USA, and Coventry, England

Ferguson Models TE-20, TEA-20, TO-20

In fall 1946, Ford Motor Company and Harry Ferguson, Incorporated, dissolved their handshake agreement that had sealed production of the Ford-Ferguson 9N and 2N tractors since 1939. Ford continued to build tractors for Ferguson into mid-1947, but after that, Ford built and distributed its Ford 8N, while Ferguson imported the TE-20 from its English plant. By 1948, Ferguson had its Detroit plant in operation, and TO-20s were rolling out the door in great numbers for the U.S. market. The TE tractors then supplied the British, Canadian, and European markets.

A 1955 Ferguson TE-20. This one was configured to operate on TVO, or Tractor Vaporizing Oil. There were also versions for gasoline, kerosene, and diesel fuel.

The TE-20 was a dead ringer for the Ford-Ferguson, right down to the paint color. There were, however, important differences incorporated by the innovative Ferguson. Rather than opening panels for access to fuel and battery, the entire hood of the "Fergie," as they came to be known, could be tilted. To insure the starter would not be engaged while the tractor was in gear, the shift lever operated the starter. The TE-20 used a Continental engine. For the TEA-20 the switch was made to a Standard Motorcar Company powerplant. Other variations were the TED-20 (tractor vaporizing oil/TVO fuel), TEH-20 (kerosene), TEF-20 (Perkins diesel). There were other minor variations, including the TET-20 (Standard Motorcar diesel).

Models and Variations	
Model	Years Built
TE-20, TEA-20	1946–1956
TO-20	1948–1951

Specifications: Ferguson TE-20

Engine: Overhead-valve four-cylinder
Bore & stroke: 3.19x3.75 inches (89.75x93.75 mm)
Displacement: 120 ci (1,966 cc)
Power: 24 belt hp
Transmission: Four speeds forward
Weight: 2,500 pounds (1,125 kg)

Above: *Even before Henry Ford and Harry Ferguson dissolved their business arrangement in 1947, Ferguson was building his look-alike TE-20 in Coventry, England. This one is equipped with a four-cylinder Standard Motors engine.*

Left, top: *A 1936–1937 Ferguson-Brown Type A, the first production tractor to incorporate a draft load-compensating three-point hitch. This tractor was the forerunner of the Ford-Ferguson 9N.*

Left, bottom: *A 1955 Ferguson TE-20 Diesel. The four-cylinder engine supplied by Standard Motors, was longer than the gasoline version, so the tractor was lengthened.*

Ferguson Models TO-30 and TO-35

The Ferguson TO-20 had been designed to compete with the Ford-Ferguson 9N and 2N. By the time of the split between Ferguson and Ford, the Ford 8N was a clear improvement and had countered most of the TO-20's advantages. In late 1951, Ferguson adopted a 129-ci (2,113-cc) Continental engine, relabeling the tractor the TO-30. The "30" indicated the maximum power available from the new engine, which was about a 5-hp advantage for Ferguson over the 8N. Other than the engine change, the tractor was the same as the TO-20.

The TO-35 of 1955 boasted 134 ci (2,195 cc), bringing power up to 33 hp. By then, Ford had been through the NAA Jubilee Series and was now into the 600 and 800 Series with 34 and 50 hp. The Fords had five forward speeds, while the TO-35 offered six. With the TO-35, Ferguson went to a gray-and-green paint scheme.

In 1953, Ferguson merged with Canadian Massey-Harris.

Models and Variations

Model	Years Built
TO-30	1951–1954
TO-35	1955–1959

Specifications: Ferguson TO-35
Engine: Overhead-valve four-cylinder
Bore & stroke: 3.3125x3.875 inches
(82.8x96.875 mm)
Displacement: 134 ci (2,195 cc)
Power: 33 PTO hp
Transmission: Six speeds forward
Weight: 3,100 pounds (1,395 kg)

Above: *A Ferguson TE-30.*

Below: *Ferguson's TE-35 of 1955 was built at the firm's Banner Lane factory in Coventry, England.*

Ford Motor Company

Detroit, Michigan, USA; Cork, Ireland; and Dagenham, England

Fordson Models F and N

Henry Ford was raised on a small farm and knew of farming's toil. Once his Model T car was a success, he turned his attention to developing tractors to ease the burden of the farmer. The Fordson Model F evolved from these early experiments and from a British program in World War I to import all available tractors to increase food production. Features of the Model F included a unit frame (where engine, transmission, and axle castings are the frame), a low weight of 2,700 pounds (1,215 kg), and a low cost—as low as $395. The F was built in the United States and Ireland.

When U.S. production was discontinued in 1928, all production was transferred to Ireland, and shortly thereafter to Dagenham, England. At the time of the transfer to Ireland, the Fordson was given a modernizing upgrade and renamed the Model N. The N was heavier, better balanced, and had more power. The power increase came from increased displacement from 251 to 267 ci (4,111 to 4,373 cc), and from increasing the speed 100 rpm. A row-crop version, designated the Fordson All-Around, was exported to the United States.

Models and Variations	
Model	Years Built
F	1918–1928
N	1929–1946

Specifications: Fordson Model N

Engine: Side-valve four-cylinder
Bore & stroke: 4.12x5.00 inches
(103x125 mm)
Displacement: 267 ci (4,373 cc)
Power: 29 belt hp (gasoline)
Transmission: Three speeds forward
Weight: 3,600 pounds (1,620 kg)

A 1925 advertisement for the ubiquitous Fordson listing a price of a mere $495.

Left, top: *Henry Ford and Son sold more tractors per year than all of the other makers combined in 1924, the year this example left the factory.*

Left, bottom: *A 1939 Fordson Model N. Fordson tractors were painted bright orange from late 1937 to mid-1939. Owner: Dennis Crossman of Walton, Dorset, Great Britain.*

Below: *A 1926 Fordson Model F. The Fordson utilized a worm-gear final drive, which gave a characteristic howling sound when under load. There was a time when 70 percent of the world's tractors were Fordsons.*

Fordson Model E27N Major

The E27N Fordson was built between 1945 and 1952, using the same basic engine that the Fordson started with in 1917. Displacement increased from 251 to 267 ci (4,111 to 4,373 cc).

Following World War II, the British Ford Motor Company completely upgraded the venerable Fordson. The new design was designated E for English, 27 for the horsepower, and N for the Ford symbol for tractors. The E27N was to have more crop clearance and a three-plow rating. The engine of the Fordson N was retained. The rear axle of the E27N used spiral bevel gears, rather than the worm-drive rear end of the F and N. After 1948, a hydraulic three-point hitch was available, but draft control was not included. Starting in 1950, a Perkins P6(TA) diesel was an option. As a testimony to the ruggedness of the basic design, the Perkins engine had almost double the power of the original engine.

There were several variations on the E27N theme: versions with and without steering brakes; with and without adjustable wheel treads; rubber or steel wheels; industrials and crawler conversions. E27Ns were painted a smart dark blue with orange wheels.

Models and Variations	
Model	Years Built
E27N	1945–1952
E27N P6(TA)	1950–1952

Specifications: Fordson E27N
Engine: Side-valve four-cylinder
Bore & stroke: 4.12x5.00 inches
(103x125 mm)
Displacement: 267 ci (4,373 cc)
Power: 27 hp
Transmission: Three speeds forward
Weight: 4,000 pounds (1,800 kg)

A lineup of Fordson E27N models on show in England. (Photograph by Robert N. Pripps)

Ford-Ferguson 9N and 2N

The 1941 version of the Ford 9N is noted for prominent chrome trim on the radiator cap, shift knob, and instrument bezels. Owner: Jack Crane of Whitestown, Indiana.

Since the end of U.S. Fordson production in 1928, Henry Ford had been dabbling with experimental tractors. In England, Harry Ferguson and gear manufacturer David Brown had joined forces in 1936 to build the first tractor with Ferguson's three-point draft-control hitch, but in 1938, Ferguson and Brown had a falling out over the size and cost of the machine. Ferguson demonstrated his Ferguson-Brown tractor and implements to Ford in the United States, resulting in a gentleman's handshake agreement wherein Ford would develop a tractor using the Ferguson system, and Ferguson would develop the implements and the dealer organization. The Ford-Ferguson 9N (9 for 1939, the year of introduction) tractor was developed using a four-cylinder engine that was half the size of the successful Ford V-8. Other car and truck parts were used where possible.

In 1942, wartime shortages led to the introduction of the 2N (for 1942) with steel wheels and without a starter or generator in order to save critical materials. After the war, rubber and copper was again available, and most 2Ns were built with starters, generators, and rubber tires, and were then much the same as the 9N. 9NAN and 2NAN models were configured for distillate fuels.

Models and Variations

Model	Years Built
9N	1939–1942
2N	1942–1947

Specifications: Ford-Ferguson 9N

Engine: Side-valve four-cylinder
Bore & stroke: 3.19x3.75 inches
   (79.75x93.75 mm)
Displacement: 119.7 ci (1,961 cc)
Power: 23 PTO hp
Transmission: Three speeds forward
Weight: 2,400 pounds (1,080 kg)

A 1946 Ford-Ferguson 2N. Although 2Ns and 9Ns are externally similar with their all-gray paint, almost twice as many 2Ns were built as the more famous 9N. Owner: Floyd Dominique of Napoleon, Ohio.

One of the earliest Ford-Ferguson 9Ns with it telltale aluminum hood, which was polished by the owner.

Ford Model 8N

Henry Ford II took over from his father in 1945. With young Henry came a new breed of business managers and a way of doing business that eschewed things like handshake agreements. Besides, accounting showed that Ford had lost about $10 million in six years of tractor sales through Ferguson. Therefore, Henry II dissolved the Ford-Ferguson agreement as of mid-1947. Ford initiated its own dealership network and manufactured its own implements to go along with an almost completely new tractor, the Ford 8N (for 1948). While the 8N featured the same styling and engine as the 9N/2N, the engine's compression was raised. A four-speed gearbox replaced the three-speed unit. The brake system, hydraulic lift, and steering were improved, and a tip-out grill (for cleaning) was added. In the last year of production, a Ford-supplied high-direct-low auxiliary transmission was an available option. 8Ns were painted light gray with red castings and wheels. Model 8NAN tractors were configured for distillate fuels.

Models and Variations

Model	Years Built
8N	1947–1952

Specifications: Ford Model 8N

Engine: Side-valve four-cylinder
Bore & stroke: 3.19x3.75 inches (79.75x93.75 mm)
Displacement: 119.7 ci (1,961 cc)
Power: 26 PTO hp
Transmission: Four speeds forward; twelve with auxiliary
Weight: 2,500 pounds (1,125 kg)

Above: *The 8N Ford can be distinguished from its predecessors by its red, cast-iron, rounded rear wheels and higher steering wheel. This one is brand new, having been remanufactured by N-Complete of Wilkinson, Indiana.*

Above: *The 1952 8N Ford is considered to be the best of the best among the 9N, 2N, and 8N, since it incorporates all of the improvements since 1939. This one was remanufactured by N-Complete of Wilkinson, Indiana.*

Left: *Advertisement for the Funk Aircraft Company of Coffeyville, Kansas, which offered six-cylinder and V-8 conversion kits for Ford's 8N and later models.*

Fordson New Major, Power Major, Super Major, New Performance Super Major, Ford 5000 Diesel

A 1952 Fordson New Major. Although "Fordson Major" is in chrome letters, these were called New Majors to differentiate them from the Fordson E27N Major predecessor.

The first all-new postwar tractor from Dagenham, England, was the E1A New Major of 1953. Design had started in 1944 with one basic engine that could be configured for diesel, gasoline, or TVO distillate. To equalize the power, the bore was larger for the diesel to increase the displacement from 199 to 220 ci (3,260 to 3,604 cc). The tractor was larger and heavier than the E27N it replaced. Hydraulic implement lift was available, but not draft control. A three-speed plus two-range transmission was provided. Tricycle and wide front ends were offered.

The Power Major came out in 1958 with a new diesel-injection system that raised power from 45 to 52 hp. In 1962, another injector improvement increased it to 54 hp. The Super Major of 1960 featured draft control, disk brakes, and sleek styling. The normal blue-and-orange paint was changed to blue and cream only for those Super Majors exported to the United States as the Ford 5000 Diesel. The New Performance Super Major was much the same, except for gear-ratio changes, hydraulics improvements, and a change to blue and gray paint.

Models and Variations		Specifications:
Model	Years Built	Fordson New Major Diesel
New Major	1953–1958	Engine: Overhead-valve four-cylinder
Power Major	1958–1961	Bore & stroke: 3.938x4.524 inches
Super Major	1961–1963	(98.5x113 mm)
NP Super Major	1963–1964	Displacement: 220 ci (3,604 cc)
Ford 5000 Diesel	1962–1964	Power: 45 hp
		Transmission: Six speeds forward
		Weight: 5,300 pounds (2,385 kg)

A 1958 Fordson Power Major. Owner: Carlton Sather of Northfield, Minnesota.

The Fordson Super Major was sold in the United States as the Ford 5000 Diesel, where it was found to be a capable and competitive tractor. The Super Major series was built from 1961 to 1964.

Fordson Dexta, Super Dexta, New Performance Super Dexta, Ford 2000 Diesel

In 1957, British Ford brought out a smaller member of its diesel tractor line called the Dexta, a word meaning "handy" or "useful." The Dexta was powered by a three-cylinder Perkins diesel engine; a gasoline version was made in limited quantities. A three-speed transmission with a two-speed auxiliary was used, providing six speeds forward and two in reverse. A draft-control three-point hitch was standard equipment. Live PTO and hydraulics were available. Paint was blue with red wheels.

A Super Dexta model was introduced in 1962. It featured a displacement increase from 144 to 153 ci (2,359 to 2,506 cc). Rated engine speed was also increased from 2,000 to 2,250 rpm, and power rose from 32 to 39 hp. A differential lock was added. Super Dextas were exported to the United States as the Ford 2000 Diesel painted blue with beige wheels. In 1963, the New Performance Super Dexta debuted. Power was increased to 45 hp by increasing the rated engine speed to 2,450 rpm.

Left: *Stablemates, a Fordson Super Major stands in front of a Fordson Dexta.*

Below: *A 1958 Fordson Power Major. Built between 1958 and 1961, the Power Major used a 220-ci (3,604-cc) Ford-built diesel with a six-speed gearbox.*

Models and Variations

Model	Years Built
Dexta	1958–1961
Super Dexta	1961–1962
NP Super Dexta	1963–1964
Ford 2000 Diesel	1962–1964

Specifications: Fordson Super Dexta
Engine: Overhead-valve three-cylinder
Bore & stroke: 3.60x5.00 inches
   (90x125 mm)
Displacement: 153 ci (2,506 cc)
Power: 39 hp
Transmission: Six speeds forward
Weight: 3,000 pounds (1,350 kg)

Ford NAA, 600, 700, 601, 701, 501 Series

A completely new tractor emerged from Ford in 1953: the Model NAA, or Jubilee. The Jubilee name commemorated Ford Motor Company's fiftieth year. The NAA was longer and heavier than the 8N and boasted new styling, but its heritage was still obvious. The basic arrangement of the tractor was retained, as was the gray and red paint. A new overhead-valve engine was used, along with a new live hydraulic system. The 1954 version had some gear-ratio changes.

The new "whiz kid" management team brought in by Henry Ford II decided for 1955 that Ford would no longer offer just one tractor. Thereafter, what had been the NAA was given the basic 600 Series number, with variations such as 620 (four-speed, no hydraulics), 630 (hydraulic three-point lift, but no PTO), 640 (four-speed, hydraulic three-point lift, PTO), 650 (five-speed, lift, non-live PTO), and 660 (five-speed, lift, live PTO). In 1956, the row-crop 700 Series was added.

In 1957, the series last digits were changed to a 1. LPG and diesels options were offered. Minor improvements were incorporated, and the 501 Series was added as an offset row-crop high-clearance tractor set up for front-mounted cultivators.

Models and Variations	
Model	Years Built
NAA	1953-1954
600 Series	1955-1957
700 Series	1956-1957
601 Series	1958-1961
701 Series	1958-1961
501 Series	1959-1961

Specifications:
Ford Model 661 gasoline
Engine: Overhead-valve four-cylinder
Bore & stroke: 3.44x3.60 inches (86x90 mm)
Displacement: 134 ci (2,195 cc)
Power: 35 hp
Transmission: Five speeds forward
Weight: 3,300 pounds (1,485 kg)

Right, top: *This 1953 Ford Model NAA Golden Jubilee is owned by the Sparks family of Shirley, Indiana. It has been in the family since new.*

Right, center: *A 1955 Ford Model 600. The 600 was almost the same as the Jubilee of 1953 and 1954, with only minor internal improvements.*

Right, bottom: *A 1960 Ford 601.*

Ford 800, 900, 801, 901 Series

A 1951 Ford Model 901 row-crop pulling a three-bottom plow. Owner: Don Artman of Monee, Illinois.

This Ford Model 971 is an LPG-fueled row-crop tractor with the ten-speed Select-O-Speed power shift transmission. Owner: Dwight Emstrom of Galesburg, Illinois.

A beautiful Ford Model 861 Powermaster, complete with wheel weights and umbrella. The 800 Series Fords were capable of 50 hp.

These tractors were essentially the same as their 600 and 700 Series counterparts, except that the engine bore was increased from 3.56 to 3.90 inches (89 to 97.5 mm). This gave these tractors an ample 172-ci (2,817-cc) displacement and put it into the 50-hp class. Gasoline, LPG, and diesel versions were available, as was the ten-speed power-shift Select-O-Speed transmission.

Again, model numbers indicated the configuration: the prefix "8" stood for a four-wheel utility type; the "9" was a row-crop. The middle number indicated the following variations:

1: Select-O-Speed, no PTO
2: Four-speed, no PTO or three-point lift
3: Four-speed, lift, no PTO
4: Four-speed, lift, non-live PTO
5: Five-speed, lift, non-live PTO
6: Five-speed, lift, live PTO
7: Select-O-Speed, lift, live PTO
8: Select-O-Speed, lift, non-live PTO

Models and Variations

Model	Years Built
800 Series	1955–1957
900 Series	1955–1957
801 Series	1958–1961
901 Series	1958–1961

Specifications: Ford 851 gasoline
Engine: Overhead-valve four-cylinder
Bore & stroke: 3.90x3.60 inches
   (97.5x90 mm)
Displacement: 172 ci (2,817 cc)
Power: 50 hp
Transmission: Five speeds forward
Weight: 3,450 pounds (1,552.5 kg)

Frick Company
Waynesboro, Pennsylvania, USA

Frick Models A and C

The Frick Model A. The more powerful Model C was also built, which had much the same appearance. Large front wheels were said to roll easier over soft ground and cause less compaction.

Frick, an old-line steam engine and threshing machine manufacturer, made two internal-combustion tractors of its own design, the Models A and C. Production of these two models began in 1918 and was discontinued in 1928. From 1928, Frick sold Minneapolis tractors made by the Minneapolis Threshing Machine Company. Frick exited the tractor business in 1930.

Frick's Model A tractor began with a rating of 12/25; this was reduced to 12/24, and then 12/20, as a result of University of Nebraska testing. An Erd four-cylinder engine was mounted crosswise in a channel-iron frame with curved rails. Exposed drive gears were used.

The 15/28 Model C used the same frame but wider wheels. A four-cylinder Beaver engine of 425 ci (6,962 cc) was used with a two-speed transmission. Otherwise, the A and C were similar in configuration and appearance.

Models and Variations	
Model	Years Built
A	1919–1928
C	1918–1928

Specifications: Frick Model A
Engine: Overhead-valve four-cylinder
Bore & stroke: 4.00x6.00 inches
    (100x150 mm)
Displacement: 302 ci (4,947 cc)
Power: 20 belt hp
Transmission: Two speeds forward
Weight: 5,800 pounds (2,610 kg)

Friday Tractor Company
Hartford, Michigan, USA

Friday Model 048 Orchard

The Friday tractor is an interesting and unique unit. First made in 1948 (hence its number designation), it used a 217.7-ci (3,566-cc) Chrysler industrial engine rated at 46 hp; in Dodge trucks of the period, this same engine was rated at 95 hp. In any case, it was one of the more powerful tractors available at the time. It was equipped with a five-speed transmission and two-speed rear axle, most likely also from Dodge. The combination gave ten forward and two reverse speeds. The speed range went from less than 2 to more than 30 mph (3.2 to 48 km/h). The Friday was designed and built for Michigan fruit growers, and made only in the orchard configuration. It was never tested at Nebraska, but was rated by the manufacturer for three 14-inch (35-cm) plows. A hydraulic system and PTO were options.

The brake system was another unique feature of the Friday. Two hand brake levers were provided to assist with steering. A single pedal brake, or service brake, was used for normal stopping. In addition, a hand-lever parking brake was provided.

The unique Friday Model 048 was based on Dodge truck components. The engine was governed to 46 hp and about 33 mph (53 km/h). By overriding the governor, 60 mph (96 km/h) was possible.

Models and Variations	
Models	Years Built
048	1948–1952

Specifications: Friday 048

Engine: Side-valve six-cylinder
Bore & stroke: 3.25x4.375 inches
  (81.25x109.375 mm)
Displacement: 217.7 ci (3,566 cc)
Power: 46 PTO hp
Transmission: Five speeds forward plus
  two-speed axle
Weight: 4,200 pounds (1,890 kg)

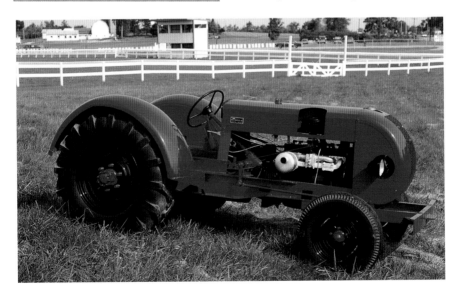

General Motors Corporation
Pontiac, Michigan, USA

Samson Sieve-Grip, Model M

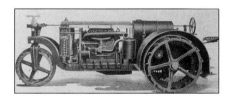

Samson's Sieve-Grip of 1914 featured a four-cylinder engine producing 12/25 hp.

William Crapo Durant, chairman and founder of General Motors, lost a chance to buy the Ford Motor Company in 1908 because of financing difficulties. Thereafter, he was determined to challenge Ford on every field of battle, including farm tractors. Durant learned Ford was developing a tractor in 1915, so he hired tractor expert Philip Rose to survey all creditable tractor makers and recommend one for purchase by GM. Rose selected the Samson Tractor Works of Stockton, California, and a deal was made.

Samson's Sieve-Grip was produced with a variety of engines from 1914 through 1917. They were low-slung, long machines with a goose-neck single front wheel and open spur-gear rear-wheel drive. The most popular version used a four-cylinder engine of 425 ci (6,962 cc), giving the tractor a 12/25 rating. The name Sieve-Grip came from the open-face rear wheels.

The $1,750 price of the Sieve-Grip made it uncompetitive when the $700 Fordson debuted in 1918, so GM moved the operation to a new plant in Janesville, Wisconsin, and brought out a new design, the Model M, which arrived in late 1918, selling for $650. It had fenders, governor, and belt pulley standard, while these were extras on the Fordson. A 276-ci (4,521-cc) engine gave the Model M a 12/20 rating. By 1922, Henry Ford had dropped the price of the Fordson to $395, and GM stockholders forced Durant to give up the tractor business.

Models and Variations

Model	Years Built
Sieve-Grip	1914–1917
Model M	1918–1922

Specifications: Samson Model M

Engine: Side-valve four-cylinder
Bore & stroke: 4.00x5.50 inches
   (100x137.5 mm)
Displacement: 276 ci (4,521 cc)
Power: 20 hp
Transmission: Two speeds forward
Weight: 3,300 pounds (1,485 kg)

The General Motors Samson Model M was built in a special new plant in Janesville, Wisconsin. It was designed as a direct and able competitor to the successful Fordson.

Graham-Paige Motors Corporation
Detroit, Michigan, USA

Graham-Bradley 503.103 and 503.104

A 1938 Graham-Bradley 503.103. Made by the Graham-Paige automobile company for exclusive sale by the Sears Roebuck catalog firm, the 503 was possibly the most stylish tractor ever built.

Founded in 1908, the Paige-Detroit Motor Car Company was a pioneer in the automotive industry. In 1928, the Graham brothers acquired the company, renaming it Graham-Paige Motors Corporation, and continued producing stylish automobiles. In 1938, a tractor was produced through an exclusive sales agreement with the giant mail-order firm, Sears, Roebuck & Company of Chicago. The tractor was called the Graham-Bradley as the Bradley name had been used by Sears for farm items for some time.

The 503.103 tricycle version was first offered in 1938. The wide-front 503.104 was introduced in 1939. Both were powered by Graham-Paige's L-head six-cylinder engine with a four-speed transmission. Rubber tires, electric starter, and lights were features. A hydraulic implement lift, PTO, and belt pulley were available. The belt pulley was downstream of the transmission and offered four speeds. The tractor had streamlined looks, and it was in fact quite racy, with a top speed of 20 mph (32 km/h).

Tractor production was interrupted in 1942 by World War II. At the end of the war, Graham-Paige's president Joseph Frazer merged the company with Henry J. Kaiser, the ship-building magnate. The resulting Kaiser-Frazer automobile company never revived tractor production.

Models and Variations

Model	Years Built
503.103	1938–1941
503.104	1939–1941

Specifications:
Graham-Bradley 503.104

Engine: Side-valve six-cylinder
Bore & stroke: 3.25x4.375 inches
   (81.25x109.375 mm)
Displacement: 218 ci (3,571 cc)
Power: 30 PTO hp
Transmission: Four speeds forward
Weight: 5,000 pounds (2,250 kg)

A Sears Roebuck and Company catalog page listing the Graham-Bradley tractor claims: "Looks like a Million and just as good as it looks."

Happy Farmer Tractor Company
Minneapolis, Minnesota, USA

Happy Farmer

One of several three-wheeled tractors of the 1915 era, the Happy Farmer was the brain-child of D. M. Hartsough, who had gained recognition for his Big Four tractor of 1911 built by the Gas Traction Company. The Happy Farmer Tractor Company was organized in November 1915. Tractors were built under contract by the H. E. Wilcox Motor Company of Minneapolis, and sold by the LaCrosse Implement Company of La Crosse, Wisconsin. After about a year, Happy Farmer, LaCrosse, and the Sta-Rite Engine Company merged to form the LaCrosse Tractor Company, which lasted to 1924.

The Happy Farmer used several engines, the most common being a two-cylinder side-by-side similar to the Waterloo Boy. Like the Waterloo Boy, the Happy Farmer had exposed valve mechanisms and drive gears. Later versions of the Happy Farmer used a wide front end. The paint scheme was orange and black early on, and later switched to orange and dark green.

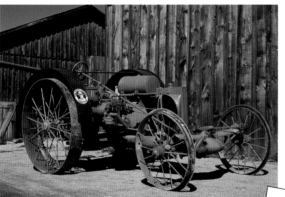

Left: *The engine of the Happy Farmer tractor was much like that of the John Deere Waterloo Boy; however, the Happy Farmer was a somewhat lighter tractor.*

Below: *An advertisement for La Crosse Tractor Company's Happy Farmer Tractor: "Every man who owns a Happy Farmer Tractor boosts for it."*

Models and Variations

Model	Years Built
Happy Farmer	1916–1924

Specifications: Happy Farmer

Engine: Overhead-valve two-cylinder
Bore & stroke: 5.00x6.50 inches
   (125x162.5 mm) early; 6.00x7.00
   inches (150x175 mm) late
Displacement: 255 ci (4,177 cc)
Power: 24 hp
Transmission: One speed forward
Weight: 4,200 pounds (1,890 kg)

Hart-Parr Company
Charles City, Iowa, USA

Hart-Parr Oil-Cooled Models

Charles Hart and Charles Parr formed their enterprise before the dawn of the 1900s. By 1901, they had made their first gas-powered tractor and coined the actual term "tractor." The Hart-Parr No. 1, like subsequent tractors of this series, used a two-cylinder, oil-cooled engine. By 1903, some fifteen variations of this original had been sold, the latest boasting 45 belt hp. A 17/30 and an 18/30 model filled out the line. By 1907, one-third of all American tractors were Hart-Parrs.

Next came the Old Reliable Model 30/60, built in 1907 and one of the most successful of the series, continuing in production through 1918. Other sizes were also built during this period.

By 1918, some company stockholders insisted that water-cooled tractors of smaller size were the wave of the future. Eventually, pioneers Hart and Parr left the company over the dispute, and the big oil-cooled monsters came to the end of their line.

Models and Variations

Model	Years Built
17/30	1903–1906
22/45	1903–1906
30/60	1907–1918
40/80	1908–1914
15/30	1909–1912
20/40	1912–1914

Specifications:
Hart-Parr Old Reliable 30/60

Engine: Overhead-valve two-cylinder
Bore & stroke: 10.00x15.00 inches
(250x375 mm)
Displacement: 2,356 ci (38,591 cc)
Power: 60 belt hp
Transmission: One speed forward
Weight: 20,500 pounds (9,225 kg)

A 1912 advertisement for Hart-Parr's oil tractors: "They will work 24 hours in the day and seven days in the week."

Hart–Parr Models 30, 20, 40

A 1926 Hart-Parr Model 20, or 12/24E. The 12/24E was an updated version of the older 10/20 model and used a two-speed transmission.

After the departure of Charles Hart and Charles Parr from the Hart-Parr Company, a line of comparably lightweight water-cooled tractors was developed. The first of these was the Hart-Parr 30, or 15/30 Type A, of 1918. It used a two-cylinder, side-by-side engine and a two-speed transmission. A water pump and a friction-driven fan were features. Slightly modified Types C and E followed through 1926 with ratings of 16/30. A Type G at 18/36 was built in 1926 and 1927. A Type H with a three-speed transmission was built from 1928 to 1930.

A smaller 10/20 followed, known as the Model 20, and there were several types made from 1921 to 1930. The best of these was the 12/24 of 1924, which was made in several versions, the 12/24E and 12/24H. A 22/40 using essentially two 10/20 engines side by side was also built.

Finally, the Model 40 28/50 was built in 1923, with production continuing to 1927. This four-cylinder outfit used two 12/24 engines side by side and could pull six plows.

Hart-Parr was absorbed by Oliver Farm Equipment Company in 1930.

Similar to John Deere, Hart-Parr used a two-cylinder horizontal side-by-side engine until 1923. This 1920 Hart-Parr 30A 15/30 is owned by David Preuhs of LeCenter, Minnesota.

Models and Variations		Specifications:
Model	Years Built	Hart-Parr Model 40 28/50
Model 30 Type A 15/30	1918–1924	Engine: Overhead-valve four-cylinder
Model 30 Type C 16/30	1924–1926	Bore & stroke: 5.75x6.50 inches
Model 30 Type E 16/30	1924–1926	(143.75x162.5 mm)
Model 30 Type G 18/36	1926–1930	Displacement: 675 ci (11,057 cc)
Model 30 Type H 18/36	1928–1930	Power: 28 drawbar hp, 50 belt hp
Model 20 10/20	1921–1924	Transmission: Two speeds forward
Model 20 22/40	1923–1927	Weight: 8,600 pounds (3,870 kg)
Model 20 12/24	1924–1930	
Model 40 28/50	1927–1930	

Huber Manufacturing Company
Marion, Ohio, USA

Huber Model 30/60 and Four Crossmotors

Huber's history stretched back into the late 1800s when it offered farm steam engines of 8, 12, and 16 hp.

Inventor Edward Huber founded his farm equipment company in 1865. During the following years, he patented more than one hundred inventions. Company activities included tractors as early as 1898, although only limited production was achieved until 1912, when the giant 30/60 was unveiled. It used a four-cylinder engine with a bore and stroke of 7.00x8.00 inches (175x200 mm). The tractor's tubular radiator carried some 95 gallons (313.5 liters) of water. The rear wheels were 8 feet (240 cm) high. These monsters were painted a light orange color.

The Waukesha-engined Huber Light Four 12/25 debuted in 1917, followed in 1921 by the Midwest-engined Super Four 14/30 and in 1922 by the Hinkley-engined Master Four 25/50. The Master Four featured a totally enclosed drivetrain. All were relatively lightweight, inexpensive designs with vertical crossmounted four-cylinder engines. Nebraska tests proved Huber's ratings to be quite conservative. Paint was still the dusty orange, changing to green later in production. They were produced into 1925.

Models and Variations

Model	Years Built
30/60	1912–1916
Light Four	1917–1925
Super Four	1921–1925
Master Four	1922–1925

Specifications:
Huber Light Four 12/25

Engine: Overhead-valve four-cylinder
Bore & stroke: 4.50x5.75 inches
  (112.5x114 mm)
Displacement: 366 ci (5,995 cc)
Power: 12 drawbar hp, 25 belt hp
Transmission: Two speeds forward
Weight: 5,200 pounds (2,340 kg)

Huber's first successful production tractor, the huge Model 30/60. Its 1,232-ci (20,180-cc) engine used 95 gallons (261 liters) of cooling water in its tubular radiator.

Huber Models 18/36, 20/40, 40/62, 20/36

Huber's New Super Four Series were conventionally configured tractors with inline engines, enclosed drives, and unit frames. The first of the series, the 18/36 of 1926, used a Sterns four-cylinder engine of 460 ci (7,535 cc) and two-speed transmission. In 1929, it was rerated at 21/39, indicating how conservative Huber ratings generally were.

The Huber Model 40/62 was rerated from 25/50 following Nebraska tests. The 40/62 was a large machine weighing almost five tons (4,500 kg).

The 20/40 came out in 1927, and was also known as the Model HK. It was rerated as a 32/45 in 1929 following Nebraska Tractor Tests. This model used a 536-ci (8,780 cc) Sterns engine. According to Nebraska tests, this tractor was actually capable of a remarkable 40 drawbar and 50 belt hp.

The 40/62 came out in 1927 as the 25/50, but was rerated following its Nebraska test later that same year. A 618-ci (10,123-cc) Sterns engine and two-speed transmission were used.

In 1929, Huber's new Light Four, as it was designated, featured a Waukesha L-head engine of 443 ci (7,256 cc) rated at a conservative 20/36. A Ricardo high-compression head was featured; this type of head was also sold aftermarket for the Fordson and others, with good results.

The 1921 Huber Super Four shown here was a crossmotor tractor that rivaled the famous Waterloo Boy in configuration and performance. The Huber Manufacturing Company made three competitive crossmotor tractors from 1917 to 1925: the Light Four, the Super Four, and the Master Four.

Models and Variations

Model	Years Built
18/36	1926–1929
20/40	1927–1941
40/62	1927–1941
20/36	1929–1935

Specifications:
Huber New Super Four 40/62

Engine: Overhead-valve four-cylinder
Bore & stroke: 5.50x6.50 inches
  (137.5x162.5 mm)
Displacement: 618 ci (10,123 cc)
Power: 40 drawbar hp, 62 belt hp
Transmission: Two speeds forward
Weight: 9,910 pounds (4,460 kg)

International Harvester Company
Chicago, Illinois, USA

International Harvester Mogul and Titan, Early Models

A 1908 International Harvester Type A Mogul. The Type A was built between 1907 and 1911. It was a gear-drive machine, as opposed to the previous friction-drive tractors from International Harvester.

The International Harvester Company of Chicago was formed in 1902 from the merger of five implement manufacturers, the McCormick Harvesting Machine Company and Deering Harvester Company being the principals. The firm immediately became the largest farm equipment manufacturer in the world. Tractor production began in 1906, and "Harvester," as the company came to be called, soon was a major player in the market. McCormick and Deering had maintained separate dealerships, so two separate tractor lines were developed: the Mogul for McCormick and Titan for Deering.

The Type A Mogul began in 1907 as a 12-hp model, but grew to develop 15 hp. Originally built with friction drive, two-speed gear drives were later incorporated. Several other sizes of Moguls were built including popular 45-hp and 60-hp jobs. There was also a 25-hp Mogul Junior.

The Type D Titan was introduced in 1910 in the 20–25-hp class. They were single-cylinder machines with huge pistons, and displacement totaled 902 ci (14,775 cc). Titan 45 and 30/60 tractors followed with two-cylinder engines.

Models and Variations		Specifications:
Model	Years Built	International Harvester Titan Type D
Mogul Type A	1907–1916	Engine: Overhead-valve single-cylinder
Mogul Junior	1911–1913	Bore & stroke: 8.75x15.00 inches
Mogul 45	1911–1917	(218.75x375 mm)
Mogul 30/60	1911–1917	Displacement: 902 ci (14,775 cc)
Titan Type D	1910–1914	Power: 20 hp
Titan 45	1911–1915	Transmission: One speed forward
Titan 18/35	1912–1915	Weight: 10,000 pounds (4,500 kg)
Titan 30/60	1915–1917	

International Harvester Mogul Type A. The Type A won in its class at the Winnipeg Motor Competition in 1909. It also won the Sweepstakes Medal for scoring the most points of any entry.

Only 259 examples of the Titan Type D, as shown here, were built between 1912 and 1915. The Type D was rated at 18 drawbar and 35 belt hp.

International Harvester Mogul and Titan, Late Models

An International Harvester Model 8/16 Mogul. More than 14,000 Model 8/16s were built between 1914 and 1917. It was replaced by the 10/20 Mogul.

In 1914, International Harvester brought out its first "lightweight" tractor, the Mogul 8/16, a single-cylinder, hopper-cooled, rugged workhorse. In 1916, a version with a larger engine was introduced, the 10/20. These tractors were characterized by an arched frame and narrow-set front wheels, allowing sharp turns. Final drive was by roller chain. The 8/16 used a single-speed transmission; for the 10/20, a two-speed unit was added.

A two-cylinder Titan 10/20 came out in 1915 in a configuration similar to that of the Mogul and using a two-speed transmission. Cooling for the Titan was by "Thermosyphon," using a large water tank mounted high on the frame. The price for these tractors was about $1,000—before competition from the Fordson forced the price down to $700, which included a P&O plow worth about $100.

Another small tractor was introduced in 1917, variously called the International or Mogul 8/16. This design was based on the then-current International trucks, and the engine was the same as that of the Model G truck. The 8/16 had a three-speed transmission and fan-cooled radiator.

Models and Variations

Model	Years Built
Mogul 8/16	1914–1917
Mogul 10/20	1916–1919
Titan 10/20	1915–1922
International (Mogul) 8/16	1917–1922

Specifications: International Harvester Titan 10/20

Engine: Overhead-valve two-cylinder
Bore & stroke: 6.40x8.00 inches (160x200 mm)
Displacement: 531 ci (8,698 cc)
Power: 20 belt hp
Transmission: Two speeds forward
Weight: 5,700 pounds (2,565 kg)

This 1919 International Harvester Titan 10/20 was a capable tractor in its day. Titan tractors were marketed through Deering dealers; Moguls through McCormick dealers.

A 1919 International Harvester Model 8/16 Junior.

International Harvester Models 15/30, 10/20, 22/36

The McCormick-Deering 15/30 was introduced to replace the Mogul and Titan and to counter the erosion of market share caused by the Fordson in 1921. The 15/30 featured an engine with ball-bearing mains, all-gear drive, and a unit frame. The seat and steering wheel were offset to the right to enhance plowing visibility. It had a foot-operated clutch and a rear PTO. The engine boasted a displacement of 382 ci (6,257 cc), and the tractor weighed 6,000 pounds (2,700 kg).

Late in 1922, Harvester introduced a smaller, lighter, and less-expensive tractor, the 10/20. It looked like the 15/30, but weighed only 4,000 pounds (1,800 kg). The 284-ci (4,652-cc) engine shared the ball-bearing mains with the 15/30. Like the 15/30—and the Fordson—it had a three-speed transmission. It was available in narrow, orchard, and industrial versions.

The Model 22/36 was an upgrade of the 15/30 that came out in 1929. Except for changes to the engine, it was the same as its predecessor. The engine bore was 0.25-inches (6.25-mm) larger, and the operating speed was increased 50 rpm.

A 1932 McCormick-Deering Model 10/20. The 10/20 was International Harvester's first response to the market inroads made by the Fordson. It was the Farmall, however, that finally beat the Fordson.

Models and Variations

Model	Years Built
15/30	1921–1928
10/20	1923–1939
10/20 Industrial (Model 20)	1923–1940
22/36	1929–1934
15/30 Industrial (Model 30)	1930–1932

Specifications:
McCormick-Deering 10/20

Engine: Overhead-valve four-cylinder
Bore & stroke: 4.25x5.00 inches
   (106x125 mm)
Displacement: 284 ci (4,652 cc)
Power: 20 belt hp
Transmission: Three speeds forward
Weight: 4,000 pounds (1,800 kg)

The driver's position on the McCormick-Deering 15/30 was offset to the right for improved plowing visibility. (Photograph by Robert N. Pripps)

International Harvester Farmall Regular, F-20, H, Super H, 300, 350

The original Farmall became known as the Farmall Regular after the F-20 and F-30 Farmalls were introduced. The Regular was the tractor that started the all-purpose tractor revolution.

Growing out of the short-term interest in "motor cultivators" from 1915 to 1918, the Farmall became the first successful production all-purpose farm tractor. The first Farmalls, sold in 1924, were capable of the draft and belt work of their predecessors, plus they had the rear PTO for powering harvesters and the crop clearance for cultivating. Thus a Farmall could replace all the horses on a farm.

Over the years, Farmalls were made in five series, four corresponding standard-tread versions and in high-crop, Orchard, and Special models. These, and their successors in this mid-size series, were two-plow-rated tractors.

A feature of the early Farmalls was cable-operated brakes linked to the steering. Regular brake pedals replaced the cables in 1939. An overhead-valve four-cylinder engine with magneto ignition was used, although LPG and diesel versions of the 350 were available. Debuting in 1939, the Raymond Loewy–styled Farmalls were strikingly beautiful and still look modern today.

Models and Variations		Specifications: International Harvester
Model	Years Built	Farmall Super H
Regular	1924–1931	Engine: Overhead-valve four-cylinder
Regular Fairway	1926–1931	Bore & stroke: 3.50x4.25 inches
F-20	1932–1939	(87.5x106 mm)
H	1939–1952	Displacement: 164 ci (2,686 cc)
Super H	1952–1954	Power: 31 PTO hp
300	1954–1956	Transmission: Five speeds forward
350	1956–1958	Weight: 4,389 pounds (1,975 kg)

Above: *A 1939 Farmall F-20. This was the last version of the F-20. Owner: Larry Gloyd of Rockford, Illinois.*

Left, top: *A 1934 Farmall F-20. Although not given a power rating by International Harvester, the F-20 delivered 16/24 hp in tests.*

Left, bottom: *The Farmall H was available in a variety of configurations. Shown here is the row-crop wide-front arrangement. This 1944 example was photographed in Dorset, England.*

The HV was a special high-clearance Farmall H. A unique front axle and chain final drives raised the HV about 10 inches (25 cm) higher than the normal Farmall H.

One of the most stylish of all farm tractors was the 1956 Farmall 300. Owner: Austin Hurst of Lafayette, California.

International Harvester Farmall F-30, M, Super M, 400, 450

The Farmall F-30 was the forerunner of the Farmall M. The one shown is a 1937 model, by which time rubber tires were a common option.

While the first Farmalls were considered two-plow tractors, this series was developed to pull three plows. Introduced in 1932, the F-30 used the same engine as the McCormick-Deering 10/20, but operated at higher rpm. The F-30 was longer and heavier than the two-plow F-20, while the steering and brake arrangement was continued from the F-20, as was the four-speed transmission. Adjustable wide-front and high-crop versions were available. In 1936, rubber tires became an option, the paint was changed from gray to red, and a hydraulic lift became available.

The F-30 became the Raymond Loewy–styled M in 1939 and featured a new 248-ci (4,062-cc) engine. In 1941, a diesel engine became available in the Model MD. The Super M and Super MD of 1952 had increased displacement and power; LPG fuel versions were also available. The transmission had five speeds, but in 1954, the M-TA was introduced with a power shift Torque Amplifier auxiliary, making it a ten-speed tractor. The 400 of 1954 and the four-plow 450 of 1956 were improvements on the basic theme designed to keep the tractor competitive.

Models and Variations	
Model	Years Built
F-30	1932–1939
M	1939–1952
Super M	1952–1954
400	1954–1956
450	1956–1958

Specifications: International Harvester Farmall Super MD

Engine: Overhead-valve four-cylinder
Bore & stroke: 4.00x5.25 inches (100x131 mm)
Displacement: 264 ci (4,324 cc)
Power: 47 belt hp
Transmission: Five speeds forward
Weight: 6,000 pounds (2,700 kg)

Left, top: *A 1952 Farmall Super M. Styled by the famous designer Raymond Loewy for 1939, the Farmalls still look modern sixty years later.*

Left, bottom: *The Farmall 450 was made from 1956 to 1958. A 281-ci (4,603-cc) engine gave it more than 50 hp. Owner: John and Mary Lou Poch of New Holstein, Wisconsin.*

Below: *The ultimate version of the original styled Farmall, the great Model MD-TA. The MD was the diesel version of the mighty M. The TA, or Torque Amplifier, allowed a power-shift half-step for each transmission ratio.*

International Harvester W-4, O-4, OS-4, Super W-4, 300 Utility, 350 Utility, 330, 340

The Farmall 340 was the row-crop version of this series; the International 340 was the utility version. Both used a 135-ci (2,211-cc) four-cylinder engine.

Despite the increasing interest in row-crop tractors in the 1930s, standard-tread machines were still in demand. The International W-4 was the standard-tread version of the Model H, replacing the 10/20 in 1940. It was equipped with the same powerplant and transmission as the H. Orchard versions—the OS-4 and O-4—were available.

The 300 Utility was the standard-tread version of the Farmall 300 row-crop. The engine was rated at higher rpm, however, giving the 300 Utility slightly more power. Like the Farmall 300, it was available with an LPG engine. The 350 Utility corresponded to the Farmall 350 row-crop, and was available in gasoline, LPG, or diesel versions.

The 330 did not have a corresponding row-crop tractor and was built in 1957 and 1958 only. Along with the International 340 (utility) and Farmall (row-crop), it used the same 135-ci (2,211-cc) engine as the International T-340 crawler. Both the 330 and 340 were available with the Torque Amplifier transmission to accompany their regular five-speed units. The 340 could be equipped with either the two- or three-point hitch.

An International Harvester McCormick-Deering W-4, the standard-tread version of the Farmall H.

Models and Variations

Model	Years Built
W-4, O-4, OS-4	1940–1953
Super W-4	1953–1954
300 Utility	1955–1956
350 Utility	1956–1958
330	1957–1958
340	1958–1963

Specifications: International Harvester 350 Utility gasoline

Engine: Overhead-valve four-cylinder
Bore & stroke: 3.625x4.25 (90.625x106 mm)
Displacement: 175 ci (2,867 cc)
Power: 41 hp
Transmission: Five speeds forward
Weight: 4,600 pounds (2,070 kg)

International Harvester W-30, I-30, W-6, O-6, OS-6, W-400, W-450, 460, 560

A 1949 W-6 International Harvester, the standard-tread version of the Farmall M, photographed working in England.

Models and Variations

Model	Years Built
W-30	1932–1940
I-30	1932–1940
W-6, O-6, OS-6	1940–1953
Super W-6	1952–1954
W-400	1955–1956
W-450	1956–1958
460	1958–1963
560	1958–1963

Specifications:
International 460 gasoline

Engine: Overhead-valve six-cylinder
Bore & stroke: 3.56x3.6875 inches
(89x92 mm)
Displacement: 221 ci (3,620 cc)
Power: 41 hp
Transmission: Five speeds forward; ten
with Torque Amplifier
Weight: 7,700 pounds (3,465 kg) with
ballast

The McCormick-Deering W-30 was a powerful work-horse.

The standard-tread version of the Farmall F-30 was the McCormick-Deering W-30. Orchard and industrial versions were also offered; the industrial version was called the I-30, or Model 30, not to be confused with the 15/30 Industrial, also known as the Model 30. The W-30 was essentially the same machine as the F-30, except that it kept the three-speed transmission when the F-30 went to four.

The W-6 had the same engine and transmission as the Farmall M, just as the Super W-6 mirrored the Farmall Super M. These models included gasoline, diesel, and LPG versions, and the Torque Amplifier auxiliary transmission. O-6 and OS-6 orchard tractors were also available.

Likewise, the W-400 paralleled the Farmall 400. Diesel and gasoline versions were offered, as was the Torque Amplifier. The same relationship existed for the W-450 and the Farmall 450.

Completely restyled for 1958, the International 460 was also available as the Farmall 460. Six-cylinder LPG, gasoline, and diesel versions were offered, all delivering about 50 hp. These engines were coupled with a five-speed transmission and Torque Amplifier.

The top-of-the-line Farmall 560 was only available as a row-crop tractor. Its standard diesel six-cylinder engine displaced 282 ci (4,916 cc); gasoline and LPG engines were also offered.

**McCormick-Deering
Triple-Power Tractors**

International Harvester A, B, C, 100, 130, 140, 200, 230, 240

The 1939 restyling of the entire Farmall line by noted industrial designer Raymond Loewy covered both form and function. Most prominent in that regard was the diminutive Farmalls A and B. These tractors were mechanically the same, but the A had a wide front, while the B had a tricycle front. The A used one long axle in the back, and one short one with the driver and steering wheel offset to the right; the B used two long axles. The driver position was the same in the two tractors, however. The A and B were excellent cultivating tractors for truck gardeners because of the visibility afforded the driver. As with other Farmalls, the upgraded version of 1952 added the "Super" appellation, making the A the Super A.

The B was replaced, in 1948, by the C, which was the same mechanically, but had an operator's platform, stood higher, and looked much larger. A Super C came out in 1952.

The 100, 130, and 140 were upgraded and restyled versions of the original A. Likewise, the 200, 230, and 240 were improved later models of the C. The 240, however, was a complete redesign with on-center steering. It was also available as the International 240 Utility.

Models and Variations	
Model	Years Built
A	1939–1953
B	1939–1947
C	1948–1951
Super A	1952–1954
Super C	1952–1954
100	1954–1956
130	1956–1958
140	1958–1979
200	1954–1956
230	1956–1958
240	1958–1962

Specifications:
International Harvester Farmall 100
Engine: Overhead-valve four-cylinder
Bore & stroke: 3.13x4.00 inches
   (78.25x100 mm)
Displacement: 123 ci (2,015 cc)
Power: 18 hp
Transmission: Four speeds forward
Weight: 3,000 pounds (1,350 kg)

Above: *The Farmall A was ideal for truck gardeners, and a whole catalog of custom implements were available. With ballast, the A could exert a drawbar pull of almost 2,400 pounds (1,080 kg).*

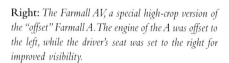

Right: *The Farmall AV, a special high-crop version of the "offset" Farmall A. The engine of the A was offset to the left, while the driver's seat was set to the right for improved visibility.*

Above: *The diminutive Farmall B weighed only 1,800 pounds (810 kg), yet it was capable of pulling a 16-inch (40-cm) plow. Although they shared the same engine, the B was capable of wider rear axle treads than the Model A.*

Left: *The Farmall C replaced the Model B in 1948; the Super C replaced the C in 1951. Owner: Mary Lou Langy of Lena, Illinois.*

International Harvester F-12, W-12, Fairway 12, I-12, O-12, F-14, W-14, Fairway 14, I-14

An unusual, wide-front Farmall F-12, as most were dual-tricycle fronts. F-12s operated on kerosene or gasoline.

Debuting in 1932, the Farmall F-12 was the one-plow version of the successful two-plow F-20 and three-plow F-30. It was originally equipped with a Waukesha engine, but an International engine was soon developed for it. A kerosene manifold and gasoline-starting system was an extra-cost option. Early F-12s had a single front wheel; dual tricycle wheels and a wide front end soon became available. The tractor was equipped with a three-speed transmission. Rubber tires were available almost from the beginning.

The F-14 replaced the F-12 in 1938. The new tractor was almost identical to the F-12, except an increase in engine speed gave the F-14 a two-plow rating. The steering wheel was mounted higher for a more comfortable position and angle. Both the F-12 and F-14 could be equipped with an implement lift.

The W-12 and W-14 were standard-tread versions of the F-12 and F-14, of which they were essentially the same, but were lower and had fixed wheel tread. There were orchard, golf course, and industrial models based on these units.

Models and Variations		Specifications:
Model	Years Built	International Harvester
F-12	1932–1938	Farmall F-14 distillate
W-12	1932–1940	Engine: Overhead-valve four-cylinder
Fairway 12	1934–1938	Bore & stroke: 3.00x4.00 inches
I-12	1934–1938	(75x100 mm)
O-12	1935–1938	Displacement: 113 ci (1,851 cc)
F-14	1938–1939	Power: 17 hp
W-14	1938–1939	Transmission: Three speeds forward
Fairway 14	1938–1939	Weight: 3,300 pounds (1,485 kg)
I-14	1938–1939	

A 1936 Farmall W-12. Only about 4,000 of this standard-tread version of the Farmall F-12 were built. Owner: Ralph Oliver of Madrid, Iowa.

A nicely restored McCormick-Deering O-12, the orchard version of the Farmall F-12 and W-12 Standard. The sweeping orchard fenders dominate its profile.

Farmall Cub, Lo-Boy, International Cub

The Farmall Cub boasted the same configuration as the Farmall A, but was smaller in size, and the rear of the Cub's fuel tank was rounded rather than teardrop-shaped.

A tiny 60-ci (983-cc) four-cylinder L-head engine provided 10 hp. Cubs were equipped with a three-speed transmission, a rear PTO or belt pulley, and steering brakes. A special mowing Cub was called the Lo-Boy. A variety of custom implements was made for the Cub, including a front-end loader. Later versions of the Cub were labeled as Internationals rather than Farmalls.

Models and Variations

Model	Years Built
Farmall Cub	1947–1958
Lo-Boy	1955–1975
International Cub	1958–1975

Specifications: Farmall Cub

Engine: Side-valve four-cylinder
Bore and stroke: 2.62x2.75 inches
(65.5x68.75 mm)
Displacement: 60 ci (983 cc)
Power: 10 hp
Transmission: Three speeds forward
Weight: 1,500 pounds (675 kg)

A Farmall Cub, with an ambitious one-bottom plow, off to do some serious work. The Cub can be distinguished from the Farmall A by its rounded gas tank. (Photograph by Robert N. Pripps)

A 1958 Farmall Cub. The little Cub used a four cylinder L-head engine of only 60 ci (983 cc).

International Harvester W-40, W-9, 600, 650, 660

Standard-tread, or wheatland, tractors were a big part of International Harvester's product line. Besides those based on row-crop tractors, this series was built solely as standard-treads. The first, the McCormick-Deering W-40, was a six-cylinder machine, technically known as either the WA-40 with a 279-ci (4,570-cc) engine or as the WK-40 with a 298-ci (4,881-cc) engine. A four-cylinder diesel tractor, the WD-40 was the first diesel wheeled tractor. Both versions were also available as industrial tractors.

The International W-9 replaced the W-40 in 1940 and featured the stylish Raymond Loewy–penned sheet metal. It used the 335-ci (5,487-cc) four-cylinder engine from the T-9 crawler. The diesel-powered WD-9, introduced in 1945, was basically the same engine beefed up to handle diesel loads. Industrial and rice versions of both the W-9 and WD-9 were available. Super WD-9 tractors had increased displacement to 350 ci (5,733 cc).

The 600 was merely a designator change for the W-9 Series to keep parallel with the other International tractors. This was true also for the 650, although a five-speed transmission was added and LPG fuel became an option.

The 660, however, was considerably different. It was completely restyled, and a Torque Amplifier was added. Six-cylinder engines were available to run on either diesel, gasoline, or LPG.

Above: *The McCormick-Deering WD-40 of 1934 was the first diesel-powered wheel tractor. It pioneered International Harvester's diesel starting system, which converted the engine momentarily to a gasoline type.*

Models and Variations

Model	Years Built
W-40	1934–1940
WD-40	1934–1940
W-9	1940–1953
WD-9	1945–1953
Super WD-9	1953–1956
600	1956–1956
650	1956–1958
660	1959–1963

Specifications:
International 660 diesel

Engine: Overhead-valve six-cylinder
Bore & stroke: 3.69x4.39 inches
    (92x109.75 mm)
Displacement: 282 ci (4,619 cc)
Power: 79 hp
Transmission: Five speeds forward plus
    Torque Amplifier
Weight: 10,000 pounds (4,500 kg)

Left: *The McCormick-Deering W-40. There were two versions of this six-cylinder tractor: the WA-40 and the WK-40. The diesel WD-40 used a four-cylinder engine.*

Massey-Harris-Ferguson, Ltd.
Toronto, Ontario, Canada

Massey–Harris Early Models

A 1913 Little Bull tractor pulls a Deere gang plow. The Bull was a twelve-horsepower, three-wheeled tractor made by the Bull Tractor Company of Minneapolis, Minnesota.

The Massey-Harris Company was formed in 1891 by the merger of two great Canadian implement makers, Massey Manufacturing Company of Toronto and A. Harris, Son & Company of Brantford, Ontario. It was not until 1917 that the new firm entered the tractor business, marketing the Big Bull tractor manufactured by the Bull Tractor Company of Minneapolis, Minnesota. The Big Bull was an early attempt at making a smaller, lighter tractor; it had three wheels but only one wheel was driven. Later, Massey-Harris took another flyer in the business with the Parrett tractor manufactured in Chicago, Illinois. The Parrett used a Buda four-cylinder engine. Neither of these ventures was successful.

H. M. Wallis, son-in-law of Jerome Increase Case, had entered the tractor business in 1902, producing the Wallis Bear, Cub, 12/20, and 20/30. Wallis was also head of the J. I. Case Plow Works, a company founded by J. I. Case separate from the J. I. Case Threshing Machine Company. Wallis tractors were built at the Case factory in Racine, Wisconsin. Massey-Harris bought the J. I. Case Plow Works (and sold the rights to the Case name to the other Case company) in 1928, and continued producing the Wallis 20/30. The Wallis Cub and subsequent Wallis and Massey tractors used Wallis's patented boilerplate unit frame.

Models and Variations		Specifications:
Model	Years Built	Massey-Harris Model 12/20
Big Bull	1917–1918	Engine: Overhead-valve four-cylinder
Parrett	1918–1923	Bore & stroke: 3.875x5.25 inches
Bear	1902–1911	(96.875x131.25 mm)
Cub	1912–1915	Displacement: 248 ci (4,062 cc)
Cub Junior	1915–1919	Power: 20 belt hp
K, OK	1919–1927	Transmission: Three speeds forward
12/20	1927–1933	Weight: 3,550 pounds (1,598 kg)
20/30	1927–1933	
Model 25	1929–1933	

In 1918, Massey-Harris tried its luck with the Buda-powered Parrett tractor. The Ontario Agricultural Museum owns this 1921 example.

The Wallis Model K was actually built by the J. I. Case Plow Works of Racine, Wisconsin, with production ending in 1927. Massey-Harris bought the Case Plow outfit in 1929 and continued many Wallis models.

Massey-Harris General Purpose 15/22

The first all-new tractor from Massey-Harris was the radical four-wheel-drive General Purpose 15/22. It was powered by a Hercules four-cylinder engine that could be configured for either kerosene or gasoline. The engine drove all four equal-sized wheels via a three-speed transmission and spur-gear final drives. These final drives used large-diameter gears on the wheels and small gears on the ends of the axles. Since this mesh was at the top, there was ample crop clearance under the axles. The front wheels pivoted for steering through Universal joints, while the rear axle swiveled around the differential input to allow for uneven terrain. The General Purpose 15/22 exhibited a drawbar pull of 95 percent of its own weight at its Nebraska test—yet it was criticized for insufficient power. A six-cylinder Hercules engine was tried in a few tractors, but even then, farmers would not pay for the complexity and lack of maneuverability of the four-wheel drive when tractors like the Farmall and John Deere A and B were available at a lower cost.

The four-wheel-drive Massey-Harris G-P came out in 1930. It was capable of pulling 95 percent of its own weight in its Nebraska drawbar pull test.

Models and Variations

Model	Years Built
General Purpose	1930–1936

Specifications: Massey-Harris General Purpose 15/22

Engine: Side-valve four-cylinder
Bore & stroke: 4.00x4.50 inches
   (100x112.5 mm)
Displacement: 226 ci (3,702 cc)
Power: 25 belt hp
Transmission: Three speeds forward
Weight: 3,400 pounds (1,530 kg)

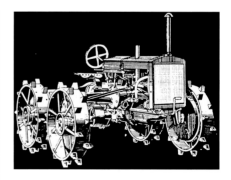

Massey-Harris's General Purpose was made in four tread widths so it could conform to a variety of different row spacings.

Massey-Harris Pacemaker, Challenger

Originally, Massey-Harris Challengers were painted gray. Owner: the Peterson family of Chesterton, Indiana.

With the demise of the General Purpose 15/22, Massey-Harris revived and modernized the old Wallis 10/20. The row-crop version was called the Challenger. It actually had a rating of 16/26, and came equipped with adjustable rear wheel treads. It continued to use Wallis's boilerplate U-frame, or unit frame. The standard-tread Pacemaker was originally much like the Wallis 10/20 when it came out in 1936. For 1937, it received some stylish sheet metal, as did the Challenger in 1938; the re-styled models were called the Twin-Power Challenger and Pacemaker, and used high-compression gasoline engines. The Twin-Power designation resulted from two governor settings of 1,200 and 1,400 rpm; the lower setting lessened the amount of wheel spin, while the higher setting worked well on the belt. Accordingly, a 24/36 rating was generated at its Nebraska test. Both rubber tires and steel wheels were available for the Twin-Power Pacemaker and Challenger. These were the last of the Wallis-type tractors.

A 1938 Massey-Harris Challenger. It was developed as a row-crop version of the Wallis 12/20 beginning in 1936. Note the boiler-plate frame pioneered by Wallis.

Models and Variations

Model	Years Built
Pacemaker	1936–1938
Challenger	1936–1938

Specifications: Massey-Harris Twin-Power Challenger

Engine: Overhead-valve four-cylinder
Bore & stroke: 3.875x5.25 inches
(96.875x131.25 mm)
Displacement: 248 ci (4,062 cc)
Power: 40 belt hp
Transmission: Four speeds forward
Weight: 5,900 pounds (2,655 kg) on
rubber tires

Massey–Harris Models 81, 20, Colt, 22, Mustang, 101 Junior, 102 Junior, 30, 33, 333

This 1950 Massey-Harris Model 22 standard-tread was an outgrowth of the Model 81 and Model 20. A Continental four-cylinder engine was used.

For 1939, Massey-Harris brought out its own original line of tractors. The smallest series, the one-/two-plow 81 through the 102 Junior, used a Continental four-cylinder L-head engine. The Model 81 was built in relatively limited numbers in both standard-tread and row-crop versions. It used the 124-ci (2,031-cc) version of the engine. In 1947, the 81 became the Model 20, and in 1950, it became the 22. Displacement was increased to 140 ci (2,293 cc) by increasing the bore. The Colt of 1954 reverted to the Continental 124-ci (2,031-cc) engine, while the Mustang used the 140-ci (2,293-cc) engine.

The Model 101 and 102 Juniors were much the same as the Model 81 through Model 22 line and were powered by the same Continental engines. Four-speed transmissions were used throughout. They were available in row-crop and standard versions and with the Twin-Power feature.

The Model 30, 33, and 333 were two-/three-plow tractors with five-speed transmissions; the 333 had a two-range shifter. The same Continental engine was used in the 30, but its bore was increased further to 162 ci (2,654 cc). The 33 and 333 used overhead-valve, four-cylinder Massey-Harris engines of 201 and 208 ci (3,292 and 3,407 cc) respectively. A limited number were equipped with diesel or LPG engines. Depth-O-Matic hydraulic three-point hitch was available on the 333.

Models and Variations		Specifications:
Model	Years Built	Massey-Harris Model 333
81	1939–1948	Engine: Overhead-valve four-cylinder
20	1947–1948	Bore & stroke: 3.6875x4.875 inches
Colt	1952–1956	(92x121.875 mm)
22	1948–1953	Displacement: 208 ci (3,407 cc)
Mustang	1954–1956	Power: 40 hp
101 Junior	1939–1946	Transmission: Ten speeds forward in two
102 Junior	1942–1946	ranges
30	1946–1952	Weight: 5,900 pounds (2,655 kg)
33	1952–1955	
333	1956–1956	

Left: *The Massey-Harris Model 81 was built in both standard and row-crop versions. The 81 row-crop as shown was a one-/two-plow tractor.*

Below, top: *A 1945 Massey-Harris 102 Junior Standard featuring Twin-Power, which provided a different rpm for belt or drawbar work.*

Below, bottom: *Massey-Harris's Model 33 tractors were offered in gasoline (shown) and diesel versions. Row-crop (shown) and standard-tread configurations were available.*

Above: *A 1942 Massey-Harris Model 81-R Standard. Standard-tread versions of the Model 81 were built from 1941 to 1946. They were used extensively as Canadian military aircraft tugs in World War II.*

A 1956 Massey-Harris Model 333 row-crop. An upgrade of the Model 33, the 333 was offered with power steering, live PTO, and a three-point hitch.

Massey-Harris Model 33 Diesel tractors came out in 1952. Shown is a 1953 row-crop. The diesel was capable of about 36 hp.

Massey-Harris Models 101, 101 Super, 102 Senior, 201 Distillate, 202

Late in 1938, Massey-Harris established the styling and paint color for its tractors for the next twenty years. Typical of the lineup were the six-cylinder 101s. These gutsy tractors used engines supplied by the Chrysler Corporation, which were versions of the tough L-head Dodge truck engine modified for Massey-Harris. The Twin-Power feature was used with governor settings of 1,500 and 1,800 rpm. A four-speed transmission was used offering speeds up to 16 mph (25.6 km/h) at 1,800 rpm. The 101 used an engine of 201 ci (3,292 cc), while the 101 Super boasted 218 ci (3,571 cc). A feature of the early 101s was the stylish louvered engine side panels; these disappeared just before World War II as they were expensive to make and hindered cooling airflow. The 102 Senior row-crop and standard tractors came out in 1945, featuring a six-cylinder Continental engine of 226 ci (3,702 cc).

The 201 Distillate and 202 (gasoline) arrived in 1941. Six-cylinder Continental engines were used displacing 330 ci (5,405 cc) for the 201 Distillate and 290 ci (4,750 cc) for the 202. Twin-Power (set at 1,700 and 2,000 rpm) was featured on these four-/five-plow standards. The 203 Distillate was an update of the 201 Distillate.

Models and Variations

Model	Years Built
101	1938–1939
101 Super	1939–1946
102 Senior	1942–1946
201 Distillate	1941–1941
202	1941–1942
203 Distillate	1942–1946

Specifications:
Massey Harris 101 Standard

Engine: Side-valve four-cylinder
Bore & stroke: 3.125x4.375 inches
  (78x109.375 mm)
Displacement: 201 ci (3,292 cc)
Power: 36 belt hp
Transmission: Four speeds forward
Weight: 3,800 pounds (1,710 kg)

Above: *A nicely restored 1941 Massey-Harris Super 101 row-crop. Twin Power was featured, governing two different engine speeds, thus reducing wheel slip when pulling and allowing more power on the belt.*

Left: *A 1941 Massey-Harris Super 101, which used a 218-ci (3,571-cc), six-cylinder engine made by Chrysler. Owner: Scott Fred of Fred Farms, Indiana.*

Massey-Harris Pony and Pacer

A 1951 Massey-Harris Pony, the firm's smallest tractor. From 1950 on, a hydraulic lift was available. Owner: Larry Darling of Michigan.

Introduced in 1948, the Pony was designed to compete with the John Deere Model L, Allis-Chalmers G, and Farmall Cub. These ultra-small tractors were popular for truck gardens and around estates, golf courses, and even on large farms, where they did chores too light for the large tractors. Although they did tasks now done by "garden" tractors, they were serious machines, built tough for farm jobs such as belt-driving a corn sheller. The Pony came equipped with a three-speed gearbox and Continental four-cylinder L-head engine of 62 ci (1,016 cc), giving it 11 PTO hp.

An improved version, the Pacer Model 16, was introduced in 1954. A Continental four-cylinder was used again, but displacement was up to 91 ci (1,491 cc). A live PTO was an option. The Pacer was not rated by the University of Nebraska, but power was estimated at 16 PTO hp. Both the Pony and Pacer weighed under 1 ton (900 kg), and both came only in the adjustable wide-front configuration.

Models and Variations

Model	Years Built
Pony	1948-1954
Pacer	1954-1957

Specifications: Massey-Harris Pony

Engine: Side-valve four-cylinder
Bore & stroke: 2.375x3.50 inches
(59.375x87.5 mm)
Displacement: 62 ci (1,016 cc)
Power: 11 PTO hp
Transmission: Three speeds forward
Weight: 1,890 pounds (850 kg)

The Massey-Harris Pony used the 62-ci (1,016-cc), L-head Continental engine, virtually the same as that used in the Allis-Chalmers G and the Farmall Cub.

Massey-Harris Models 44, 44-6, 44 Special, 444

A 1947 Massey-Harris 744PD fitted with an English-made Perkins diesel engine. The 744PB was an English-market variation of the 44.

The first of Massey-Harris's post–World War II tractors was the standard-tread 44, arriving in 1946. The row-crop version was introduced in 1947. These simple, straightforward machines became known for dependability and reliability. In 1948, a diesel version was added to the lineup. Both the diesel and gasoline versions used the same basic Massey-Harris 260-ci (4,259-cc) engine; the diesel version produced about 5 hp less than the gasoline version.

The 44-6 version came out in 1947 in both row-crop and standard-tread configurations. It was essentially the same as the 44, except for the change to the 226-ci (3,702-cc), six-cylinder Continental engine.

The 44 Special was a 1955 upgrade of the original 44. The Massey engine was increased to 277 ci (4,537-cc), putting out more than 50 hp. A five-speed gearbox, live PTO, and hydraulic lift were standard.

The 444 had the same basic engine as the 44 Special. A two-speed auxiliary power-shift transmission, along with the standard five-speed, gave ten forward speeds and two in reverse. Power steering was an extra-cost option, and an LPG version was also available.

Models and Variations

Model	Years Built
44	1946–1955
446	1947–1957
44 Special	1955–1957
444	1956–1958

Specifications:
Massey-Harris 44 Special

Engine: Overhead-valve four-cylinder
Bore & stroke: 4.00x5.50 inches
  (100x137.5 mm)
Displacement: 277 ci (4,537 cc)
Power: 45 hp
Transmission: Five speeds forward
Weight: 5,800 pounds (2,610 kg)

A beautifully restored Massey-Harris 44-O. The 44-O was the orchard version of the reliable post–World War II standard and row-crop Masseys. (Photograph by Robert N. Pripps)

Massey-Harris Models 55, 555

The four-/five-plow Massey-Harris 55 of 1946 was built in Racine, Wisconsin.

Massey-Harris brought out the big, standard-tread Model 55 in 1947. These large standards—such as the John Deere R, Case 500, and International Harvester W-9—were mostly plowing tractors, popular in the Great Plains. Five plow bottoms were common loads. The 55 was a 60-hp machine available to run on either gasoline or diesel; an LPG version was later added. A hand-operated clutch was standard equipment. Special Western and Riceland versions were also available.

Like the 55, the Model 555 used a Massey-Harris 382-ci (6,257-cc) engine and was available in gasoline, diesel, or LPG versions. A four-speed gearbox was used. Hand or foot clutches were optional, but power steering was standard.

Models and Variations

Model	Years Built
55	1947–1955
555	1956–1958

Specifications:
Massey-Harris 55 Diesel

Engine: Overhead-valve four-cylinder
Bore & stroke: 4.50x6.00 inches (112.5x150 mm)
Displacement: 382 ci (6,257 cc)
Power: 60 hp
Transmission: Four speeds forward
Weight: 7,800 pounds (3,510 kg)

Production of the Massey-Harris Model 55 gasoline, shown here, began in 1946. The 55 was only available as a standard-tread machine. A diesel model followed in 1949.

Massey-Ferguson MF-35, MF-50, MF-65, MF-85, MF-88

Massey-Ferguson's MF-85 of 1959 was a 60-hp tractor available in both row-crop and standard configurations. Gasoline or diesel engines were featured.

When Harry Ferguson merged his company into Massey-Harris in 1953, the Ferguson TO-35 was already in the works. Under Massey-Harris-Ferguson, new sheet metal and a red-and-gray paint job were added in 1955, making it the MF-35. A three-cylinder Perkins diesel became optional alongside the existing 134-ci (2,195-cc) Continental gasoline engine. The Perkins 152-ci (2,490-cc) diesel was the same as that used in the Fordson Super Dexta.

The MF-50 arrived in 1958. It was essentially the same as the MF-35, using the same Perkins or Continental engines and six-speed transmissions. An LPG version of the MF-50 was available.

The MF-65 used a 203-ci (3,325-cc) Perkins four-cylinder diesel or a 176-ci (2,883-cc) Continental four. An LPG version of the Continental was also offered. A six-speed transmission was standard, while a power-shift two-speed auxiliary was available. A high-clearance configuration was offered.

The MF-85 was available in tricycle, high-clearance, and utility configurations. A 242-ci (3,64-cc), four-cylinder Continental engine was standard, but diesel and LPG were options.

Introduced in 1959, the MF-88 featured a 277-ci (4,537-cc) Continental diesel, which boosted power over 63 PTO hp. A four-speed gearbox with a two-range shifter gave eight ratios forward and two in reverse.

Models and Variations	
Model	Years Built
MF-35	1955–1957
MF-50	1958–1964
MF-65	1957–1965
MF-85	1958–1961
MF-88	1959–1961

Specifications:
Massey-Ferguson MF-65
Engine: Overhead-valve four-cylinder
Bore & stroke: 3.578x4.375 inches
   (89.45x109.375 mm)
Displacement: 176 ci (2,883 cc)
Power: 44 PTO hp
Transmission: Twelve speeds forward with
   power shift
Weight: 4,100 pounds (1,845 kg)

A 1963 Massey-Ferguson 95 Super, which was a Minneapolis-Moline G in Massey-Ferguson colors.

English-built Massey-Ferguson 35s had different, more rounded sheet metal from that of their U.S.-built counter-parts. The red paint scheme was adopted shortly after the Massey-Harris and Ferguson merger.

Minneapolis-Moline Company
Minneapolis, Minnesota, USA

Moline Universal

The Minneapolis-Moline Company was formed in 1929 by the merger of three old-line farm equipment companies: the Moline Plow Company of Moline, Illinois; Minneapolis Steel & Machinery Company of Minneapolis, Minnesota; and Minneapolis Threshing Machine Company of Hopkins, Minnesota. By pooling the resources of the parent firms, the new firm was able to withstand the financial pressures of the Great Depression.

In 1919, Moline Plow had developed the world's first truly all-purpose tractor, the Universal. The tractor's roots lay with the Universal Tractor Company of Columbus, Ohio, which Moline Plow bought in 1915. With this acquisition came a two-cylinder, two-wheel concept that required special sulky implements to support the back end and to provide a place for the operator. By 1918, Moline had redesigned and re-engined the Universal with one of its own four-cylinder engines. The Universal is noted for being the first tractor to include a starter and lights as standard. It was also unusual with its articulation steering, an electric governor, and concrete wheel weights. It did not, however, survive the great tractor price war of the 1920s when Henry Ford and International Harvester cut prices below costs to maintain market share.

Above: *The Moline Universal was one of the first all-purpose tractors. It was also the first to use articulation steering. This one was built in 1918.*

Right: *The Moline Universal, besides all its other innovations, was the first farm tractor to offer a starter and lights.*

Models and Variations	
Model	Years Built
Universal	1918–1923

Specifications: Moline Universal
Engine: Overhead-valve four-cylinder
Bore & stroke: 3.50x5.00 inches
   (87.5x125 mm)
Displacement: 192 ci (3,145 cc)
Power: 27 belt hp
Transmission: One speed forward
Weight: 3,400 pounds (1,530 kg)

Minneapolis Threshing Machine 40/80, 35/70, 20/40, 22/44, 17/30

The first of a long and famous line of Minneapolis-Moline tractors was originally sold as the Minneapolis 40/80. After testing at the University of Nebraska in 1920, it had to be down-rated to 35/70.

The Minneapolis 17/30 used a vertical four-cylinder engine of 496 ci (8,124 cc) mounted crosswise. A Type B change in 1922 lengthened the tractor slightly to improve steering.

With roots going back to 1874, Minneapolis Threshing Machine (MTM) was a key player in the threshing machine and steam engine businesses. It entered the internal-combustion tractor business in 1911, selling tractors designed and built by others. MTM went on to produce a successful line of machines using four-cylinder engines of its own design.

The 40/80 was the first MTM tractor. First built in 1912, it was a giant weighing more than 11 tons (9,900 kg). It retained many of the chassis characteristics of the Minneapolis steamers, including chain-and-windlass steering and a cooling system capacity of more than 50 gallons (190 liters) of water. In 1920, the 40/80 was submitted to the Nebraska tests; as a result, it was rerated and re-named the 35/70. As such, it remained in production until the merger of 1929.

The 20/40 debuted in 1914. It was the same configuration as the 35/70, but used a 727-ci (11,908-cc), four-cylinder L-head engine rather than the 35/70's overhead-valve type. The 20/40 was replaced by the 22/44 in 1920. The new tractor had an overhead-valve engine of 791 ci (12,957 cc) and weighed 6 tons (5,400 kg). Production continued into 1927.

The smaller, more conventional 17/30 debuted in 1920 and was carried into the merger of 1929.

Models and Variations		Specifications: Minneapolis Threshing Machine 35/70
Model	Years Built	
40/80	1912–1920	Engine: Overhead-valve four-cylinder
35/70	1920–1929	Bore & stroke: 7.25x9.00 inches
20/40	1914–1920	(181.25x225 mm)
22/44	1920–1927	Displacement: 1,486 ci (24,341 cc)
17/30	1920–1929	Power: 74 hp
		Transmission: One speed forward
		Weight: 22,500 pounds (10,125 kg)

Minneapolis Steel & Machinery TC-40, TC-60, TC-25, TC-15

Minneapolis Steel & Machinery (MSM) was formed in 1902 and was an early player in the steam engine and internal-combustion engine businesses. Agricultural tractors came under investigation in 1910, but it was not until 1911 that a machine of the firm's own design was ready for production. MSM named its models the Twin City tractors. The first was the Twin City TC-40. It was improved in 1913 and was rated at 40/65 hp at the Nebraska test in 1920. The TC-40 was powered by the company's own four-cylinder overhead-valve engine of 1,590 ci (26,044 cc). It weighed in at 25,500 pounds (11,475 kg).

A Twin City 40 of 1916, built by Minneapolis & Machinery. It was rated at 40 drawbar and 65 belt hp.

The TC-60 of 1913 was built along the same lines. It was powered by a six-cylinder engine of 2,229 ci (36,511 cc) and was rated as a 60/90 machine, weighing a whopping 28,000 pounds (12,600 kg). The cooling system contained 116 gallons (440 liters) of water.

The TC-15 also appeared in 1913, powered by a 496-ci (8,124-cc), four-cylinder engine. The TC-15 was available with several engines and radiator configurations over the years.

Next came the TC-25, a 16,000-pound (7,200-kg) tractor rated at 25/45 hp. It used a four-cylinder engine of 982 ci (16,085 cc). It was also much like the TC-40 and TC-60 in configuration.

This behemoth Twin City TC-60 from Minneapolis Steel & Machinery was intended to replace the big steam engines of its day. It was mainly used for Great Plains plowing.

Models and Variations		Specifications: Minneapolis Steel & Machinery Twin City TC-60
Model	Years Built	
TC-40	1911–1924	Engine: Overhead-valve six-cylinder
TC-60	1913–1920	Bore & stroke: 7.25x9.00 inches
TC-15	1913–1917	(181.25x225 mm)
TC-25	1913–1920	Displacement: 2,229 ci (36,511 cc)
		Power: 90 hp
		Transmission: One speed forward
		Weight: 28,000 pounds (12,600 kg)

Minneapolis Steel & Machinery TC 16/30, TC 12/20, TC 20/35, TC 17/28, TC 27/44, TC 21/32

1919 Twin City 12/20

12-20 H.P., 1,000 r.p.m., 4-cylinder vertical engine mounted longitudinally. Ignition, high-tension magneto with impulse starter; cast-iron frame, unit construction; sliding-gear transmission; final drive, enclosed spur gear; belt pulley side mounted, 650 r.p.m.; forward speed, 2.2 to 2.9 m.p.h.

The 12/20 Twin City tractor of 1919 featured a four-cylinder engine.

By 1918, MSM officials saw the handwriting on the wall: The days of the big tractors were over. Production of the heavyweights continued until 1924, but MSM made a radical departure in tractor design with the Twin City TC 16/30 of 1918. It used a totally enclosed chassis and looked like a low-slung automobile. It featured a two-speed gearbox and a four-cylinder L-head engine of 589 ci (9,648 cc). A starter and lights were optional.

The more-conventional TC 12/20 was introduced in 1919. It was the first tractor to use four valves per cylinder. The engine was a four-cylinder overhead-valve type of 340 ci (5,569 cc). It, too, used a two-speed transmission. It was redesignated as the 17/28 in 1927 following a Nebraska test.

The TC 20/35 was essentially the same design as the 17/28, but larger. It was re-rated as the TC 27/44 in 1929 and, having survived the Minneapolis-Moline merger, was built through 1935. The TC 27/44 used a four-cylinder sixteen-valve engine of 641 ci (10,500 cc).

The last of the MSM designs, the TC 21/32 F came out in 1929, featured a three-speed transmission and 381-ci (6,241-cc) engine. Production ended in 1934.

A 1918 Twin City 16/30. The success of the Fordson tractor led Minneapolis Steel & Machinery, maker of the Twin City line, to come out with this smaller competitor.

Models and Variations		Specifications: Minneapolis Steel &
Model	Years Built	Machinery Twin City TC 21/32
TC 16/30	1918–1920	Engine: Overhead-valve four-cylinder
TC 12/20	1919–1927	Bore & stroke: 4.50x6.00 inches
TC 20/35	1920–1929	(112.5x150 mm)
TC 17/28	1927–1934	Displacement: 381 ci (6,241 cc)
TC 27/44	1929–1935	Power: 39 hp
TC 21/32	1929–1934	Transmission: Three speeds forward
		Weight: 6,500 pounds (2,925 kg)

Top: *The Twin City 27/44 was also identified as the Model AT and was built from 1929 to 1935. This model was originally rated at 20/35, but up-rated following testing.*

Above, left: *The Twin City 17/28 was essentially the same as the 12/20 that came out in 1919. Testing at the University of Nebraska allowed up-rating.*

Above, right: *The last of the Minneapolis Steel & Machinery designs, the 21/32 came out in 1929, the year of the merger into Minneapolis-Moline. The 21/32 was also designated the FT.*

Left: *A beautifully restored Twin City 21/32. Owner: Leo Andea of Dryden, Michigan.*

Minneapolis-Moline Universal MT, MTA, KTA, YT

The 1935 Minneapolis-Moline MTA Universal. It was upgraded from the Universal M in 1934. Tractors from Minneapolis-Moline during this period also carried the Twin City trademark.

After the merger of 1929, M-M continued to produce Twin City tractors, but they also bore M-M trademark. The first original M-M design was the Universal MT of 1931. This 4,900-pound (2,205-kg), tricycle all-purpose tractor used a four-cylinder, 284-ci (4,652-cc), overhead-valve engine and three-speed gearbox. In 1934, the MT was upgraded to the MTA. A high-compression gasoline head was an option, as were high-speed gears for rubber tires.

Also in 1934, the KT Kombination 11/20 was replaced by the improved KTA. Besides the universal, or row-crop, version, an orchard version was available. These versions of the KTA used the same 284-ci (4,652-cc) engine as the Universal M and MTA.

The YT was not actually produced but several prototypes were built and tested, and are now in the hands of collectors. The tractor design was unusual in that it had a two-cylinder engine that was basically the back half of a four-cylinder R engine. The YT's 83-ci (1,360-cc) engine produced about 14 hp, which would have made the tractor competitive with the Farmall F-12 and other small tractors of the time.

Models and Variations		Specifications:
Model	Years built	Minneapolis-Moline Universal MT
MT	1931–1934	Engine: Overhead-valve four-cylinder
MTA	1934–1937	Bore & stroke: 4.25x5.00 inches
KT	1930–1934	(106.25x125 mm)
KTA	1934–1938	Displacement: 284 ci (4,652 cc)
YT	1937 (Prototypes only)	Power: 25 hp
		Transmission: Three speeds forward
		Weight: 4,900 pounds (2,205 kg)

The rare Minneapolis-Moline YT never actually went into production. Its engine, a two-cylinder, was half of the Model R engine.

Minneapolis–Moline Models UT, U, UB

Minneapolis-Moline Model UTS (standard). The UT featured a five-speed transmission. Even though it was a standard-tread tractor, the rear tread was adjustable over a 5.5 inch (13.75 cm) range.

The interesting UT/U/UB Series used the same rugged 284-ci (4,652-cc) engine as the MTA. This series debuted in 1938, following the restyling project of 1937, wherein the striking Prairie Gold-and-red color scheme was adopted. The UT Series included the standard-tread UTS and the row-crop UTU three-plow tractors. By 1949, the series was called simply the U Series.

The UB Series models came out in 1954. They were the same as the kerosene/distillate-burning U, except high-compression heads for gasoline and LPG fuels were added. The LPG version achieved 50 hp in its Nebraska test.

Model U variations remained in production, still with the same engine and five-speed gearbox, through 1957.

Models and Variations

Model	Years Built
UT Series	1938–1949
U Series	1949–1957
UB Series	1954–1957

Specifications: 1938 Minneapolis-Moline Twin City UTS gasoline

Engine: Overhead-valve four-cylinder
Bore & stroke: 4.25x5.00 inches (106.25x125 mm)
Displacement: 284 ci (4,652 cc)
Power: 42 hp
Transmission: Five speeds forward
Weight: 5,800 pounds (2,610 kg)

Above: *Minneapolis-Moline pioneered the use of LPG as a fuel. This tractor is a 1951 Model U Type U (LPG) owned by Ernest Weissert.*

Right: *This 1948 Minneapolis-Moline Model UTC (Cane) was the same as the UT, except for its high stance. It used a high-arch front axle, and fenders were not offered.*

Left: *The Minneapolis-Moline Model UDLX was one of the first farm tractors to have an enclosed cab. It could do 40 mph (64 km/h) on the road.*

Minneapolis–Moline Model UDLX Comfortractor

The most famous of the U Series was the UDLX, also known as the U-Deluxe and Comfortractor. Designed to be a tractor that farmers could drive to town after it had spent the day working in the field, its top speed was an amazing 40 mph (64 km/h). The UDLX featured items like a shift-on-the-fly five-speed transmission, windshield wipers, high- and low-beam headlights, taillights, cigarette lighter, heater, speedometer, and seating for three.

Under the skin the tractor was basically a Model UTS. While the enclosed cab was comfortable, the lack of hydraulics meant the back door had to be kept open in order to reach implement levers. The tractor was not practical for other than pulling jobs, as there was no belt pulley or PTO. The UDLX was less than optimum on the highway as well, since it did not have sprung axles. Even at low speeds, it tended to waddle like a duck. Where the UDLX really shone was in the service of the custom thresher. The long-distance trips pulling the threshing rig between jobs could be made in relative comfort and at reasonably high speeds. In the end, only about 150 of these stylish, but not really practical, tractors were built, and today they are one of the most admired collectible vintage tractors of all time.

Above: *A 1938 Minneapolis-Moline UDLX Comfortractor. Basically a M-M Model UTS under the stylish skin, the Comfortractor was intended to be a farm tractor that could work the fields as well as be driven to town.*

Models and Variations	
Model	Years Built
UDLX	1938–1941

Specifications:
Minneapolis-Moline UDLX Comfortractor

Engine: Overhead-valve four-cylinder
Bore & stroke: 4.25x5.00 inches (106.25x125 mm)
Displacement: 284 ci (4,652 cc)
Power: 42 hp
Transmission: Five speeds forward
Weight: 4,500 pounds (2,025 kg)

Minneapolis–Moline Models J, Z, R Series

The Minneapolis-Moline Twin City J was a truly remarkable tractor for 1934. The 196-ci (3,210-cc), four-cylinder engine was of the F-head type, meaning that the exhaust valves were in the block whereas the intake valves were in the head. A five-speed transmission gave the J a competitive advantage, however. The row-crop version, called the Universal or JT, did not use the Chicken Roost steering arm of the earlier MT, but a worm-and-sector setup in the pedestal. Clamped, adjustable-spread rear wheels were also featured. A JTS standard-tread model was offered as well from 1936 to 1937.

The Model Z debuted in 1937 as the first of the "Visionlined," styled M-Ms, sporting the new Prairie Gold-and-red colors. A feature of the Z Series was that the cylinder head could be removed, and spacers could be added or removed to adjust the compression ratio. Thus, if a farmer wanted the additional power of gasoline fuel, the higher compression would make better use of it. The Z used a smaller, 186-ci (3,047-cc) engine.

The Model R used the same engine as the Z but displaced only 165 ci (2,703 cc) and governed at a slower speed. A cab, like that of the UDLX, was an option. It was available in row-crop and standard-tread versions.

Models and Variations	
Model	Years Built
J Series	1934–1938
Z Series	1937–1956
R Series	1939–1954

Specifications: 1951 Minneapolis-Moline Model R gasoline

Engine: Overhead-valve four-cylinder
Bore & stroke: 3.625x4.00 inches
  (90.625x100 mm)
Displacement: 165 ci (2,703 cc)
Power: 26 hp
Transmission: Four speeds forward
Weight: 3,400 pounds (1,530 kg)

Above: *The Minneapolis-Moline Model Z enjoyed popularity from 1937 to 1956. In the 35-hp class, it was available after 1949 as the ZA. Shown is a 1950 ZAU (Universal).*

Left: *A Minneapolis-Moline Model R. Horizontal valves operated by long rockers facilitated maintenance with less disassembly. The R used the same engine as the Z, but governed slower.*

Above: *A Minneapolis-Moline J Standard, which had all the features of the Universal, except for the non-adjustable wheel treads.*

Left, top: *The ZB version of the Minneapolis-Moline Model Z series was offered from 1954 to 1956. A four-cylinder engine of 206 ci (3,374 cc) was used.*

Left, bottom: *The Model R Minneapolis-Moline could be equipped with an optional Comfortractor-type cab. The Model R was in the 26-hp class.*

Minneapolis-Moline GT, GTA, GTB, GTC, GB, GBD

In May 1939, the big standard-tread Model GT, weighing 9,445 pounds (4,250 kg) and one of the heaviest wheel tractors of the time, underwent testing at the University of Nebraska. It produced 54 belt hp from its four-cylinder, overhead-valve, 403-ci (6,601-cc) engine and four-speed transmission. The GT was modernized as the GTA in 1942, and again in 1947 as the GTB. The same engine, now turning faster, produced 63 hp on gasoline in the GTB, which came equipped with a five-speed gearbox.

The GTC was the same as the GTB, except its 403-ci (6,601-cc) engine was equipped for burning LPG fuel. It developed 68 hp.

The GB, another improvement that used the same four-cylinder engine, was introduced in 1954. The GBD, or GB Diesel, also came on the scene in 1954. It had an M-M six-cylinder Lanova-type diesel of 426 ci (6,978 cc). All were equipped with five-speed transmissions.

Models and Variations	
Model	Years Built
GT	1939–1942
GTA	1942–1947
GTB	1947–1954
GTC	1951–1953
GB	1954–1959
GBD	1954–1959

Specifications:
Minneapolis-Moline GBD
Engine: Overhead-valve six-cylinder
Bore & stroke: 4.25x5.00 inches
　　(106.25x125 mm)
Displacement: 426 ci (6,978 cc)
Power: 63 hp
Transmission: Five speeds forward
Weight: 8,200 pounds (3,690 kg)

Right, top: *The big Minneapolis-Moline Model GTC burned LPG fuel and developed 68 hp. It was one of the heaviest wheel tractors of the time with a working weight of around 12,000 pounds (5,400 kg).*

Right, center: *A 1955 Minneapolis-Moline Model GB with its 403-ci (6,601-cc), four-cylinder engine. A running mate of the GB was the Model GBD, with a 426-ci (6,978-cc), six-cylinder diesel.*

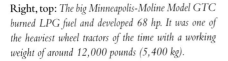

Right, bottom: *The Minneapolis-Moline Model GT used a four-cylinder engine of 403 ci (6,601 cc) and a four-speed transmission.*

Minneapolis–Moline Models BF and V

A rare example of a Minneapolis-Moline Model V. This little tractor was derived from the 1939 Cletrac-General GG.

The little BF tractor had a long and unusual history. It began life in 1939 as the Cletrac-General GG made for the Cleveland Motor Plow Company of Cleveland, Ohio, by the B. F. Avery Company of Louisville, Kentucky. In original form, it had a single front wheel, was powered by a 123-ci (2,015-cc) Hercules four, and weighed 2,700 pounds (1,215 kg). Avery took over selling the tractor in 1945 as the Avery Model A, and displacement was increased to 133 ci (2,179 cc) shortly thereafter. This tractor became the M-M BF in 1951 upon Minneapolis-Moline's takeover of B. F. Avery. It was a two-plow tractor with hydraulics and interchangeable single, dual-tricycle, or adjustable wide fronts. The rear tread was also adjustable.

A variation of the BF was the Model V, a lightweight outfit of similar configuration, but with a wide front and using a Hercules four-cylinder engine of 65 ci (1,065 cc). It tipped the scales at 1,800 pounds (810 kg). Production of both models continued through 1955.

Models and Variations

Model	Years Built
BF	1951–1955
V	1951–1955

Specifications: Minneapolis-Moline Model V

Engine: Side-valve four-cylinder
Bore & stroke: 2.625x3.00 inches
  (65.625x75 mm)
Displacement: 65 ci (1,065 cc)
Power: 12 belt hp
Transmission: Three speeds forward
Weight: 1,800 pounds (810 kg)

Oliver Corporation
Chicago, Illinois, USA

Oliver Hart–Parr Models 18/28 and 18/27

The Oliver Corporation began life as the Oliver Farm Equipment Corporation in 1929, the result of a merger of five related companies, including the Hart-Parr Company of Charles City, Iowa, and the Oliver Chilled Plow Company of South Bend, Indiana. Since Hart-Parr had a history of making creditable tractors since 1901, tractors following the merger were called Oliver Hart-Parrs.

In 1930, the Oliver Hart-Parr 18/28 was introduced with a vertical 281-ci (4,602-cc), four-cylinder engine, three-speed transmission, and conventional standard-tread design. It was capable of handling two 14-inch (35-cm) plows—three in some soils. Early ads identified this tractor as the Oliver Hart-Parr 2-3.

Also in 1930, Oliver Hart-Parr brought out a row-crop version of the standard-tread 18/28 called the 18/27: Since tractors were known by their ratings in those days, the numbers of the row-crop were altered in order to avoid confusion although the engine and transmission were the same for both. The 18/27 was originally built with a single front wheel; later, dual tricycle front wheels were used. Rear wheels for the 18/27 were a new Oliver design, called skeleton, or "Tip-Toe," wheels. These tractors were the forerunners of the Oliver 80 Series.

Models and Variations	
Model	Years Built
18/28	1930–1937
18/27	1930–1937

Specifications:
Oliver Hart-Parr 18/28
Engine: Overhead-valve four-cylinder
Bore & stroke: 4.125x5.25 inches
   (103x131.25 mm)
Displacement: 280 ci (4,586 cc)
Power: 30 hp
Transmission: Three speeds forward
Weight: 3,825 pounds (1,721 kg)

Above: *Oliver entered the row-crop, all-purpose tractor business in 1930 in a big way with the Oliver Hart-Parr 18/27. This one was built in 1932.*

Right: *Two restored Oliver Hart-Parr tractors: on the left, a 1930 18/27 row-crop; on the right, a 1930 18/28 standard. Owner: Dave Preuhs of LeCenter, Minnesota.*

Oliver Hart-Parr Models 28/44 and 90

The latest machinery offering from Oliver Hart-Parr, including several 18/28 tractors, at the 1934 Minnesota State Fair's Machinery Hill.

Models and Variations

Model	Years Built
28/44	1930–1937
90	1937–1952

Specifications:
Oliver Hart-Parr 28/44

Engine: Overhead-valve four-cylinder
Bore & stroke: 4.75x6.25 inches
   (118.75x156.25 mm)
Displacement: 443 ci (7,256 cc)
Power: 50 hp
Transmission: Three speeds forward
Weight: 6,400 pounds (2,880 kg)

In 1930, Oliver Hart-Parr presented a new tractor called variously the Model A, Model 3-5, and after testing at Nebraska, the 28/44. In this test, the 28/44 was shown to be able to pull 80 percent of its own weight. This three-/five-plow machine was built only as a standard-tread machine, at the firm's Charles City, Iowa, facility. The 443-ci (7,256-cc), four-cylinder engine was coupled to a three-speed transmission. The kerosene-burning engine was a Waukesha design, but it was built completely by Oliver, including the castings.

By 1937, this tractor was modernized and redesignated the Model 90. The same engine was used, but it had an improved high-pressure lubrication system. Also, a self-starter, generator, and fly-ball governor were added. Both gasoline and kerosene fuel versions were available. Other differences between the 90 and the previous 28/44 were that the 90 had a four-speed transmission and rear-mounted PTO. The 90 was sold in Canada as the Cockshutt 90.

A 1936 Oliver 28/44, the forerunner of the successful Oliver 90. It was capable of handling a five-bottom plow.

Oliver Models 70, 77, Super 77, 770

A remarkable new tractor was introduced by Oliver in 1935, the six-cylinder Model 70. The 70 designation represented the gasoline octane rating required for the high-compression (HC) engine; a low-compression (KD) kerosene-burning engine was also available, although both displaced 200 ci (3,276 cc). This tractor was one of the first to use stylish sheet metal to appeal to buyers. It had both a self-starter and lights as options, and was easier to drive than previous models. The 70 was available in row-crop, standard-tread, and orchard versions. In 1937, the Oliver 70 was updated and restyled as part of the Fleetline Series with the green-and-red color scheme. Six-speed transmissions were made standard on all models.

In 1947, another revision was made when the New Fleetline Series emerged: The Model 70 then became the Model 77. Gasoline and distillate engines were available at first, but a diesel soon replaced the distillate engine. An LPG engine was also available. The Super 77 was much the same, although an adjustable wide-front configuration was added.

The 770 introduced new styling and a new two-tone green color scheme. The engine choices were the same, except the governed rpm was increased. A Power-Booster power-shift torque amplifier was available.

Left: *In 1937, Oliver introduced the Fleetline Series, which included this stylish Oliver 70. The louvered side panels are removed to show the smooth-running six.*

Below: *Brochure for the Oliver 70 Orchard and Grove model.*

Models and Variations

Model	Years Built
70	1935–1937
70 Fleetline	1937–1948
77	1947–1954
Super 77	1954–1958
770	1958–1967

Specifications: Oliver 770

Engine: Overhead-valve six-cylinder
Bore & stroke: 3.50x3.75 inches
   (87.5x93.75 mm)
Displacement: 216 ci (3,538 cc)
Power: 50 hp
Transmission: Six speeds forward; twelve
   with Power-Booster
Weight: 5,500 pounds (2,475 kg)

Above: *One of the most dramatic leaps in tractor technology ever is represented by this 1936 Oliver Hart-Parr 70. The six-cylinder engine was designed to run on 70-octane gasoline.*

Right: *The row-crop Fleetline Oliver 70 was also available in the standard-tread version shown. All models of the Fleetline Series were equipped with six-speed transmissions.*

New Fleetline styling and a double numbering system was introduced by Oliver in late 1947. Shown is a nicely restored Oliver 77 Standard.

In another upgrade, Oliver introduced its Super Series in 1954. Shown is a 1955 Super 77 Diesel owned by Ken Pollesch of Ripon, Wisconsin.

Oliver Models 80, 88, Super 88, 880

The Oliver 80 was introduced in 1937 for the 1938 model year. The 80 was an outgrowth of the Oliver Hart-Parr 18/27 and 18/28 tractors of 1930–1937. When introduced, the 80 was unstyled and looked much the same as its predecessors. The four-cylinder engine was also the same, except that the bore for the kerosene version was 4.5 inches (112.5 mm), while that of the gasoline version was 4.25 (106.25 mm), equalizing the power output at 38 hp. In 1940, a diesel became available.

The 88 came out in 1947 in Fleetline livery. This was changed to New Fleetline styling in mid-1948, coinciding with Oliver's 100th anniversary. A 231-ci (3,784-cc) displacement was used for the six-cylinder gasoline and diesel engines, but the distillate version had a larger bore, yielding 265 ci (4,341 cc).

The first Oliver tractor to top 50 drawbar hp was the Super 88 of 1954. The 265-ci (4,341-cc) six-cylinder engine was used for gasoline and diesel fuels; the distillate engine was dropped. Other changes for the Super Series included the absence of engine side panels and green, rather than red, wheels.

The new 880 of 1958 bristled with improvements: More powerful engines, coupled with the Power-Booster torque amplifier and the Power-Traction three-point hitch, made the 880 much more capable.

All models in these series were sold in Canada under the Cockshutt banner.

The Oliver 80 was sold in the unstyled configuration, as shown here, until 1947. A standard-tread version of the 80 is shown; row-crops were also offered.

Models and Variations

Model	Years Built
80 Unstyled	1938–1947
88 Fleetline	1947–1948
88 New Fleetline	1948–1954
Super 88	1954–1958
880	1958–1963

Specifications Oliver 88 HC

Engine: Overhead-valve six-cylinder
Bore & stroke: 3.50x4.00 inches (87.5x100 mm)
Displacement: 231 ci (3,784 cc)
Power: 41 hp
Transmission: Six speeds forward
Weight: 5,300 pounds (2,385 kg)

A 1940 Oliver 80, which was an outgrowth of the Oliver Hart-Parr 18/27 and 18/28. It was offered with either a gasoline- or kerosene-powered four-cylinder engine.

This Oliver 88 Standard may be an antique, but it is still in the harness. Its smooth-running six-cylinder engine gave it four-plow capability.

Oliver Models 60, 66, Super 66, 660

The Oliver Super 66 sported a larger engine than its predecessors, the 60 and 66 Series tractors. Also new was a six-speed transmission and an optional diesel. This 1955 Super 66 is owned by Sam Lulich III of Mason, Wisconsin.

To offset competition from other lightweight tractors, such as the Allis-Chalmers B and Farmall A, Oliver introduced the compact Model 60 in 1940. It was a scaled-down version of the 70 and 80 tractors, although it used a four-cylinder engine, rather than the six. Both gasoline and distillate engines were available, and the transmission had four speeds. Row-crop and standard-tread models were offered. In Canada, it became the Cockshutt 60.

The 66 came out in 1947 as a 1948 model. Gasoline, diesel, and LPG engines of 129 ci (2,113 cc) were offered, as was a 144-ci (2,359-cc) distillate-burning version. All were in the 18-hp range.

Next came the Super 66 in 1954 with a four-cylinder diesel or gasoline engine of 144 ci (2,359 cc) and six-speed gearbox. A three-point hitch with Hydra-Lectric lift was used. Row-crop and standard-tread versions were optional, as was a live PTO.

Introduced in 1959, the 660 was restyled and improved over the Super 66. Both the gasoline and diesel versions displaced 155 ci (2,539 cc). Row-crop types were offered in single wheel, dual-tricycle, or adjustable wide fronts. Rear wheels were power adjustable for tread width. Double disk brakes were standard equipment. Power steering was optional.

Models and Variations

Model	Years Built
60	1940–1948
66	1948–1954
Super 66	1954–1958
660	1959–1964

Specifications:
Oliver Super 66 Diesel

Engine: Overhead-valve four-cylinder
Bore & stroke: 3.50x3.75 inches (87.5x93.75 mm)
Displacement: 144 ci (2,359 cc)
Power: 34 hp
Transmission: Six speeds forward
Weight: 4,000 pounds (1,800 kg)

An Oliver 60 Row Crop (wide-front). The Oliver 60 used a four-cylinder engine of about 18 hp and a four-speed transmission.

Oliver Models 99, Super 99, Super 99 GM, 950, 990, 995

The Oliver 99 began life in 1932 as the 99 Industrial Special High-Compression. Except for the high-compression gasoline engine, it was like the 90. Later, agricultural versions were made as the Thresherman's Special and Special Riceland. The 99 completely replaced the 90 in 1952. It then went from the four-cylinder engine to the six, and a diesel was added. The 99 also received styling treatment at that time. This series was only available in standard-tread configuration.

The Super 99 replaced the 99 in 1957. It was available with the six-cylinder gasoline engine or the six-cylinder Oliver diesel, both of which displaced 302 ci (4,947 cc). The Super 99 GM used a three-cylinder General Motors supercharged two-cycle diesel in place of the Oliver unit. Both tractors used a six-speed transmission with a torque converter as an option.

The 950 was a restyled Super 99 using the same gasoline or diesel six-cylinder engine. The 990 replaced the Super 99 GM, and was the same except the governed speed was raised from 1,600 to 1,800 rpm. It was also restyled to reflect the current corporate theme. The 995 was the same as the 990, except the Lugmatic torque converter was added. Governed speed was raised to 2,000 rpm.

Above: *A truly awesome machine, the Oliver Super 99 GM used a three-cylinder, two-cycle, supercharged General Motors 3-71 engine and a six-speed transmission. Working weight was more than 15,000 pounds (6,750 kg).*

Models and Variations	
Model	Years Made
99	1932–1957
Super 99	1957–1958
Super 99 GM	1957–1958
950	1958–1961
990	1958–1961
995	1958–1961

Specifications: Oliver 995

Engine: Supercharged two-cycle three-cylinder
Bore & stroke: 4.25x5.00 inches (106.25x125 mm)
Displacement: 213 ci (3,489 cc)
Power: 85 hp
Transmission: Six speeds forward with torque converter
Weight: 11,000 pounds (4,950 kg)

Left: *The 1953 Oliver 99 Diesel was powered by an Oliver-built six-cylinder diesel engine. Owner: Charlie Lulich of Mason, Wisconsin.*

Oliver Models Super 44 and 440

The Oliver Super 44 Utility was the smallest Oliver. It was quite capable, however, with its 140-ci (2,293-cc) Continental engine. This was the only L-head engine used by Oliver or Hart-Parr.

The Super 44 was a lightweight utility tractor that originated in 1957 in the Nichols & Shepard Company plant in Battle Creek, Michigan, one of the firms that later merged to form Oliver. After the merger, however, production was transferred to Charles City, Iowa. The Super 44 was powered by an L-head, 140-ci (2,293-cc) Continental engine, the same engine used in the Cockshutt 20 and other small tractors. This was the only L-head, or side-valve, engine ever used by Oliver or Hart-Parr. The Super 44 was fitted with a four-speed transmission. It also had an integral, compact, built-in hydraulic system for controlling the three-point hitch or remote cylinders. The tractor used a high-clearance frame with drop boxes to drive the rear wheels. The steering wheel was offset to the right to provide better visibility for the operator when cultivating delicate plants.

The 440 model signaled merely a designation change to make it the same as others in the line; otherwise it was essentially unchanged. The Super 44 and 440 found work mostly with truck gardeners, but some also were used to mow highway ditches.

Models and Variations

Model	Years Built
Super 44	1957–1958
440	1960

Specifications: Oliver Super 44

Engine: Side-valve four-cylinder
Bore & stroke: 3.20x4.40 inches (80x110 mm)
Displacement: 140 ci (2,293 cc)
Power: 16 hp
Transmission: Four speeds forward
Weight: 2,000 pounds (900 kg)

Oliver Models Super 55, 550, 500

Oliver's answer to the Ford N Series tractors, the Super 55 used a six-speed transmission and the same 144-ci (2,359-cc), four-cylinder engine as the Oliver Super 66.

The Super 55 was the first true utility-configuration tractor from Oliver. It offered either a gasoline or diesel engine of 144 ci (2,359 cc), integral hydraulics, and a draft-control three-point hitch. Front and rear wheel tread was adjustable. A six-speed transmission rounded out the features, making this one of the most useful tractors ever made. In sixth gear, travel speed was almost 15 mph (24 km/h) at 2,000 rpm.

The 550 was a restyled and improved version of an already great tractor. Displacement was increased to 155 ci (2,539 cc) for more power. Weight was up almost a half ton (450 kg). Either fixed or adjustable wheel treads were offered; power-adjustable rears were an option. A live PTO with two speeds (540 and 1,000 rpm) was standard equipment. Lights, belt pulley, swinging drawbar, and a comfy seat were options. An industrial version of the 550 was offered with a loader and backhoe. Agricultural 550s were sold in Canada under the Cockshutt banner.

The Oliver 500 was manufactured for Oliver by the David Brown Company of Meltham, Huddersfield, England. It was a two-/three-plow machine with a 33-hp four-cylinder engine and a six-speed transmission. A hydraulic three-point hitch with draft control was standard.

Models and Variations

Model	Years Built
Super 55	1954–1958
550	1958–1975
500	1960–1963

Specifications: Oliver 550 Diesel

Engine: Overhead-valve four-cylinder
Bore & stroke: 3.625x3.75 inches
  (90.625x93.75 mm)
Displacement: 155 ci (2,539 cc)
Power: 45 hp
Transmission: Six speeds forward
Weight: 4,150 pounds (1,868 kg)

Oliver 1800 Series and 1900 Series

Three models—the 1800A, B, and C—make up the 1800 Series, which made its debut in 1960. Each step incorporated improvements in the engine and ergonomics. All were six-plow machines available for LPG, gasoline, or diesel fuels. They were equipped with six-speed transmissions, although Hydra-Power Drive torque amplifier gave twelve forward and four reverse speeds. Row-crop, wheatland, and four-wheel-drive versions were available. Features included Hydra-Lectric three-point hitch, tilt-telescope steering wheel, and power steering.

An Oliver 1600 Diesel.

The 1900 Series also came in A, B, and C versions starting in 1960. These were eight-bottom tractors. The powerplant was a General Motors 4-53 two-cycle supercharged four-cylinder diesel of 212 ci (3,473 cc). These were the first Oliver tractors to exceed 100 hp. Wheatland, row-crop, and four-wheel drives were offered. The standard-tread, or wheatland, tractors had a unique splash panel between the rear fender and hood. A six-speed transmission with the Hydra-Power Drive partial-range power-shift torque amplifier was standard. Options and features were the same as those of the 1800 Series.

Models and Variations		Specifications: Oliver 1900B 4WD
Model	Years Built	Engine: Supercharged two-cycle four-
1800A	1960–1962	cylinder
1800B	1962–1963	Bore & stroke: 3.875x4.50 inches
1800C	1963–1964	(96.875x112.5 mm)
1900A	1960–1962	Displacement: 212 ci (3,473 cc)
1900B	1962–1963	Power: 101 hp
1900C	1963–1964	Transmission: Twelve speeds forward
		Weight: 13,000 pounds (5,850 kg)

Cockshutt's 1800 was actually a badge-engineered Oliver 1800 painted in Cockshutt colors for the Canadian market.

Oliver Cletrac OC-3, OC-18, OC-6, OC-12, OC-4, OC-15

Rollin White, of sewing machine and steam car fame, founded the Cleveland Motor Plow Company of Cleveland, Ohio, in 1917. He later renamed the company Cleveland Tractor Company, and it was known as Cletrac for short. Cletrac produced a line of crawler tractors (and one wheeled tractor) until 1944, when the firm was purchased by Oliver. It was at that time that Oliver changed its name to simply Oliver Corporation. A new identification scheme called for all Cletrac model names to begin with "OC" for Oliver Cletrac.

The smallest was the OC-3, which used a Hercules four-cylinder engine of 123 ci (2,015 cc). The OC-4 used gasoline or diesel Hercules three-cylinder engines of 130 ci (2,129 cc).

The OC-6 was a derivation of the Oliver 77. It used the 194-ci (3,178-cc) six-cylinder gasoline or diesel engine. The OC-12 utilized a Hercules six of 339 ci (5,553 cc) for gasoline or 298 ci (4,881 cc) for diesel.

A six-cylinder Hercules engine of 529 ci (8,665 cc) powered the OC-15, a crawler in the 70-hp class. The all-new OC-18 was the largest with a 130-hp Hercules six-cylinder engine of 895 ci (14,660 cc).

In 1960, Oliver was taken over by the White Motor Corporation of Cleveland, Ohio, thus completing the circle for Cletrac. White discontinued crawler production in 1963.

Models and Variations

Model	Years Built
OC-3	1951–1955
OC-18	1951–1963
OC-6	1954–1963
OC-12	1954–1963
OC-4	1956–1963
OC-15	1956–1963

Specifications: Oliver Cletrac OC-18 diesel

Engine: Overhead-valve six-cylinder
Bore & stroke: 5.375x6.00 inches (134.375x150 mm)
Displacement: 895 ci (14,660 cc)
Power: 130 hp
Transmission: Four speeds forward; eight with power shift
Weight: 35,000 pounds (15,750 kg)

A 1919 advertisement for the Cleveland Tractor Company's Cletrac: "The tide has turned. The big demand today is for the small tank-type tractor."

An Oliver Cletrac Model HG. Oliver crawlers were originally the products of Cleveland Tractor Company (Cletrac). The HG designation was changed to OC-3 (for Oliver-Cletrac) in 1951.

The Cletrac-General Model GG was the only wheel tractor made by Cletrac. It was marketed by Cletrac in the United States and by Massey-Harris in Canada. In 1942, the design was sold to B. F. Avery.

Rock Island Plow Company

Rock Island, Illinois, USA

Heider Models 12/20, 15/27, 9-16 and Rock Island Plow 18/35, 15/25

A Rock Island Heider 12/20. Rock Island Plow bought the rights to the Heider Brothers's tractor in 1916. J. I. Case purchased Rock Island Plow in 1937.

The Rock Island Plow Company was founded as Buford & Tate in 1855. R. N. Tate had once been a partner of John Deere in the plow business. The Rock Island name was taken by the firm about 1882, by which time it was a general manufacturer of tillage equipment. The firm began selling tractors made by the Heider Manufacturing Company of Carroll, Iowa, which had been formed by brothers Henry and John Heider in 1903. Sales were good, so Rock Island Plow (RIP) bought out Heider in 1916. The Heider name was retained until 1927, when the 18/35 was brought out bearing Rock Island's name.

The Heider 12/20 used a Waukesha four-cylinder engine of 429 ci (7,027 cc) and a single-speed drive. It weighed about 6,000 pounds (2,700 kg). The tractor was of conventional four-wheel design with an automobile-type hood and radiator. In 1924, a Waukesha engine of 479 ci (7,846 cc) was employed, along with a friction drive, and the machine became known as the 15/27.

The smaller Heider 9/16 also used a continuously variable friction drive, giving a infinite number of ratios. A 325-ci (5,324-cc) Waukesha four-cylinder engine provided power. This two-ton (1,800-kg) machine could pull a two-bottom plow.

The Rock Island 18/35 used a four-cylinder Buda engine of 381 ci (6,241 cc). A variation rated at 15/25 used a 325-ci (5,324-cc) Waukesha. These machines used a two-speed transmission.

Models and Variations	
Model	Years Built
12/20	1916–1926
15/27	1924–1927
9/16	1916–1929
18/35	1927–1936
15/25	1929–1937

Specifications: Rock Island Plow 18/35

Engine: Side-valve four-cylinder
Bore & stroke: 4.50x6.00 inches
  (112.5x150 mm)
Displacement: 381 ci (6,241 cc)
Power: 37 hp
Transmission: Two speeds forward
Weight: 4,700 pounds (2,115 kg)

Sawyer-Massey Company
Hamilton, Ontario, Canada

Sawyer-Massey Models 22/45, 20/40, 27/50, 11/22, 17/34, 12/25, 18/36

The Sawyer-Massey Model 20/40. Made in Hamilton, Ontario, this model was built between 1916 and 1921. Tractors by the firm were discontinued in the great tractor price wars of the early 1920s.

Models and Variations

Model	Years Built
22/45	1911–1917
20/40	1916–1921
27/50	1918–1922
11/22	1918–1920
17/34	1918–1920
12/25	1920–1922
18/36	1920–1922

Specifications:
Sawyer-Massey Model 27/50

Engine: Overhead-valve four-cylinder
Bore & stroke: 6.25x8.00 inches
   (156.25x200 mm)
Displacement: 982 ci (16,085 cc)
Power: 50 hp
Transmission: One speed forward
Weight: 17,500 pounds (7,875 kg)

Although there was no corporate connection between Sawyer-Massey and Massey-Harris, the Massey family had bought into the Sawyer firm in 1892. Sawyer-Massey was founded in 1836 by John Fisher and Calvin McQuesten to build threshers and steam engines. L. D. Sawyer, an employee, took over the company when Fisher died in 1856, naming the firm after himself. The Massey family bought into the company, intending to add the Sawyer steam traction engines to complete the Massey-Harris product line. In 1908–1910, tractor trials in Winnipeg, Manitoba, showed the internal-combustion tractor to be rapidly overtaking the steam traction engine in performance and popularity. When Sawyer announced its intentions of expanding its steam-engine business, the Masseys opted out. Sawyer-Massey continued with the name, and instead of steam, it entered the gas tractor market aggressively. Sawyer-Massey continued in the business until the tractor price war of 1922 brought on by Ford and International Harvester; Sawyer-Massey then went into road-building equipment.

The first gas tractor from Sawyer-Massey was the 22/45 of 1911, which became the 27/50 by 1918. A 20/40 came out in 1916. In 1918, an 11/22 and 17/34 were added to the product line. By 1920, these were rerated as the 12/25 and the 18/36.